EDGAR CAYCE'S STORY OF THE OLD TESTAMENT

Edgar Cayce, the twentieth century's most astoundingly accurate prophet, had the psychic gift. In a state of self-induced trance, Cayce, a man of little formal education, predicted such future events as the discovery of the Dead Sea Scrolls and the development of the laser beam. He was also capable of diagnosing illnesses that were beyond the knowledge of contemporary physicians—often for people thousands of miles away.

But outstanding among all his accomplishments as a clairvoyant, mystic and prophet was his ability—through psychic readings as well as in his life teachings—to make the Bible live!

Here are Edgar Cayce's profoundly magnificent revelations about God's love, reincarnation, man's spiritual role and the true meaning of the Old Testament.

From Solomon's Glories to the Birth of Jesus

EDGAR CAYCE'S
STORY OF THE OLD TESTAMENT

From Solomon's Glories to the Birth of Jesus

(Formerly titled: *Man the Messiah*)

ROBERT W. KRAJENKE

A.R.E. Press • Virginia Beach • Virginia

A.R.E. Press
215 67th Street
Virginia Beach, VA 23451-2061

Cover design by Richard Boyle

Contents

And it shall come to pass afterward that I will pour out my spirit upon all flesh; and your sons and your daughters shall prophesy, your old men shall dream dreams, your young men shall see visions; And also upon the servants and upon the hand-maidens in those days will I pour out my spirit. . . . And it shall come to pass that whosoever shall call on the name of the Lord shall be delivered; for in mount Zion and in Jerusalem shall be deliverance, as the Lord has said to the remnant whom the Lord has called.

(Joel 2:28, 29, 32)

In the days of old, when there were those developments of man as to his attempts to understand his relationships to the Maker, warnings were given again and again as to what would be the experiences of individuals who professed one thing and lived another, or who attempted to use amiss that which was given them. And these came to pass in the experiences and in the generations of those peoples so directed.

These came about in the manners indicated, though not always at the times or periods as had been FELT or expected by individuals. For, oft such expressions are found in dealing with such, that "his day and generation has not been completed," yet in a little while there comes the opportunity.

Then there came that period in man's activity in which it was proclaimed that no longer it would be in this temple or in this mountain that there would go out the message to the people, or to their gatherings here or there, but lo it would be written upon their hearts—so that the old men should dream dreams, the young men should see visions, the maidens should proclaim the acceptable year of the Lord. (3976–25)

Synopsis
of *From Joshua to the Golden Age of Solomon*

Man is meant to be the ruler of whatever sphere he occupies, whether it be in the earth or in dimensions of consciousness in other realms. (281–16)

From Joshua through Solomon, led by divinely inspired leaders, the children of Israel overcame all hardships and threats of subjugation and annihilation by pagan adversaries, only to fall into the binding snares of their own selfishness. But the cycle unfolds and the pattern is built which demonstrates the truth of man's destiny—that man is meant to be a king. His spirit is royal, his soul a birthright. Israel, the microcosm of humanity, developed the ideal king whose legacy, through his son, was a reign of splendor, supremacy, and peace.

The monarchy was an inevitable part in the pattern of man's destiny, the reflection of a cosmic principle which cannot fail to manifest or be recognized by seekers of God. Those who search for truth through faith in God will become aware of their own souls, that "image of God" given to man in the beginning. It is the soul which enables man to be "the ruler of whatever sphere he occupies."

Although God's people forced the monarchy into a premature development by "sinful" demands (1 Samuel 8:12)—fear, greed, impatience, and unbelief—they were feeling the evolutionary, drawing pull of the Spirit.

Saul was given the first opportunity. He was raised up through the demands of the people. Many factors, including his past incarnations, put him in that position. Had he lived up to the divine requirements, the heritage of an eternal throne would have come through his house and in his name. (1 Samuel 13:13) The people forced the monarchy into an early existence, and the king thrust upon the stage was ill-suited for his role. This is a part of man's lesson and a part of the drama.

When Saul failed, David was next. The idea and ideal met. Saul was the choice of the people, David was chosen by God.

David provided the pattern for the ideal king—or man—of the future. David knew God and God knew him. The meeting ground was within David, within the holy of holies—*his soul!* Knowing God was within as David did, it was natural that he yearned to express it outwardly, and made plans to build the great temple.

The golden age of Solomon was another natural consequence of David's relationship with God. Solomon built from the plans and patterns developed by David.

Under Solomon the three phases of man—body, mind, and soul—found unparalleled avenues of expression.

The *soul,* or *spiritual* aspects, were expressed through the temple and its lofty and exalted ritual and worship.

The glories of the *mind* were shown in "Solomon's wisdom," which was not the stamp of one man, but of an era—and aura—that permeated the whole kingdom.

On the level of the *body,* all the desires of the flesh were realized in a period of unparalleled ease and luxury for the ruling class.

It took Israel many generations to build its kingdom, and it may take an individual many incarnations to achieve his ideal, yet "He who perseveres to the end shall wear the crown."

From Joshua to Solomon, man learned he could be king. He could even demand it. But unless his demands were pure, they would bring his own destruction.

Unless firmly grounded in spiritual ideals, the desire for material things will blot out our awareness of our souls. Solomon inherited his father's unified kingdom, but not his stability of purpose or his spiritual vision. Solomon's desire for material things led to the dissolution of the kingdom and the downfall of Israel.

The story is not complete in Solomon. He was the fulfillment of another cycle in a pattern moving toward completion.

Man still had to learn that the kingdom was not of this world, nor was the glory to be for self.

Foreword:
World Affairs and the Bible

. . . for they [periods of history] will be
seen to come in cycles . . . for, as in energy,
there is seen the relativity of space and force
as is begun, and as same continues to vibrate,
that one law remains. Whenever it vibrates in
the same vibration, it shows as the same thing.
That's deep for you, yes. (254–47)

O, ye say, this is not new! Neither is
thy present disturbance, nor thy presence
hope, nor ANYTHING! For, even as He
said, "There is nothing new under the sun."
What is has been, and will be again.
(3976–27)

From 1930 through 1944 a remarkable series of
twenty-nine clairvoyant readings was given by Edgar
Cayce on world affairs.* Significant portions from these
readings are included in this volume for the additional
clarification they give on the meaning of the Bible.
These readings offer a psychic's commentary on a tur-
bulent and shattering era, interpreting the causes of
war, depression, and civil strife, with prophecies of

---

*These discourses are catalogued under the case number 3976
in the A.R.E. library.

earth change, revolution, and economic upheaval, and with predictions and promises concerning the rise of a new order and a new age based upon universal, spiritual happenings.

In short, as man approached the year 2000, he would pass through the complete Old Testament cycle of "the latter days" with all its threats, warnings, promises, and hopes.

The network of global events of the thirties and forties and the forecasts Cayce gave up to the year 2000 were reviewed and revealed as the effects of man's compliance or rejection of two basic spiritual ideals: *We are our brother's keeper* and *love of neighbor as of self.* The one unchanging law and principle, the one source, foundation, and resonating factor in the story of man is "thou shalt love the Lord thy God, thy neighbor as thy self." This is the basis of all spiritual law. (3976–14)

The words of the Old Testament prophets, which Cayce voiced, stressed, and paraphrased in the world affairs readings, are still valid because the cycles and patterns of man's history are unchanged. The language of his readings are replete with quotes from the Old Testament, as if Cayce in his clairvoyant consciousness could only suggest the significance of our contemporary history by its relativity to the Bible.

The Old Testament pattern was repeating itself. Why? Because man had not yet learned fully to love his brother.

Yet for those who can learn to love, even through an era of destruction, of suffering and pain as the effects of man's selfishness sweep over the earth, a new age is promised, a new testament, a new covenant is offered as it was then and is now and will forever be.

Introduction:
The Coming is from Within

In the Old Testament, men waited for the coming of a messiah. Today, Christians look for the return of the Christ. It is the same hope, the same waiting, a deep yearning for the same experience—*Completion*—the time when our earthly trials and tribulations end and all God's promises are realized and complete.

But how, we might ask, will the Lord come to those who await His Coming? The Edgar Cayce readings stress the inward experience.

The real coming is not when He returns, but when we do. God never left us. He is as much present as He ever was in the Bible days. His laws and covenants are eternal. "If ye will be my people, I will be your God." Christ said *He* would be with us always (Matthew 28:20), therefore He never went away. Man has wandered from the realization of His Presence, thus has lost one of the most precious birthrights God has given.

The Old Testament, in its most universal meaning, is the story of a fulfillment and a promise by God —to bring a blessing to all mankind. The soul we know as The Christ took it upon Himself to be that blessing. Through all His incarnations in the earth He reflected the ideals of service and self-sacrifice, manifesting the love and power of God until He was so at-one with the God-within that it became inevitable that men accept Him as the saviour and messiah. He had the abilities to demonstrate and prove His Sonship—and thus, to show us ours.

Yet the Jews did not accept Jesus as messiah, for the promised age of peace did not follow His coming, as prophesied. Some Christian thinkers say it will be the Christ of the Second Coming, the resurrected and glorified Christ that will be the messiah acceptable to the Jews, for a thousand years of peace shall follow His coming.

The Cayce readings stress that Jesus is the saviour in that He set the example and pattern by which all humanity can know the experience of the Christ, the messiah, abiding within.

What bars us from this realization? What are the biggest distractions, the greatest obstacles? It is in the Bible, it is the story of man—these must be overcome: selfishness, fear, hate, jealousy, lack of faith, lack of love. As seekers after God, we struggle with the same influences and forces as did the Israelites in their efforts to develop the pattern for a perfected humanity. We confront daily the same temptations and illusions as Jesus did in all His incarnations, whether as Adam, Enoch, Melchizedek, Joseph, Joshua, Jeshua, or Jesus.

What is a saviour? Someone who can make God's love real to another. And how do we make God real to another? By first knowing Him ourselves, as this reading indicates.

From the world affairs series, we find:

As to the material changes that are to be as an omen, as a sign to those that this is shortly to come to pass—as has been given of old, the sun will be darkened and the earth shall be broken up in divers places—and *then* shall be *proclaimed*—through the spiritual interception in the hearts and minds and

souls of those that have sought His way—
that *His* star has appeared, and will point the
way for those that enter into the holy of
holies in themselves. For, God the Father,
God the teacher, God the director, in the
minds and hearts of men, must ever be *in*
those that come to know Him as first and
foremost in the seeking of those souls; for He
is first the *God* to the individual and as He
is exemplified, as He is manifested in the
heart and in the acts of the body, of the individual, He becomes manifested before men.
(3976–15)

An earlier reading in the same series tells us how
to find Him. By looking within. The reading speaks
of a process and the direct experience of knowing.

Seek first to know within self that which has
prompted thee, and when thou hast set thine
house in order, when thou hast made thine
peace with thine own conscience (that would
smite thee, if ye will look within your own
heart), then may ye find the answers that will
come to every soul that seeks. For, as He
has given to those of old, He is the same
yesterday, today, and forever. Think not as
to who will ascend into heaven to bring down
comfort and ease to thine own aching heart,
or who will go over the seas to bring that
which may be of a recompense within thine
own experience, but lo! ye shall find it in
your own heart!
    Thus has the lawgiver given, and thus
has He said who has set the way to make the
intercession for man: "I will not leave thee
comfortless, if ye will seek to do my bid-
dings." (3976–14)

We are living in Bible times, for all time is God's time—and all life is, in its essence, spiritual.

The readings make it extremely clear how relevant the Bible is today. When passages were recommended for Bible study in the readings, often the counsel was to read them ". . . as if the writer, as if the Father was *speaking direct* to the ENTITY, to SELF!" (1231–1)

> Know that these words are speaking to self, and that they are from the living God. (3406–1)

> This is the divine speaking as to the self. (5241–1)

The Cayce readings can help us, not just to a knowledge of the Christ, not just to a stronger belief and faith in Christ, but to the experience *of* the Christ, of *being* a Christ—Christ on the *inside*, as a part and portion of the individuality and personality of our being—as well as knowing the universality of the Christ "without."

The Only Begotten Son of God is a Spirit—the Christ Spirit, the Christ that is within every soul. From this Spirit, our universe, our world, and all created things have come into being. It was the Spirit of the Christ in the hearts and minds of the Children of Israel that guided them through the long years of their history —and it is this same Spirit beckoning us, calling to every soul to complete and fulfill the pattern. When mankind can reach this point, all wars of every kind shall cease, no tears will flow, and joy and harmony shall reign everywhere.

When the Christ was fully realized and manifested in the physical life of the man Jesus, one phase in Israel's long commitment was finished—man had a Way, a star, a light to guide him—but until men and women everywhere have developed their own spirits and *MAN* is the Messiah, Israel and the Christ's work will never be complete.

Until we know the fullness of His spirit within us, we are Old Testament figures living out our chapter in the search for Truth. The Bible is not a finished piece of work. We are still completing its meaning. When we reach the state when we are transformed and "made anew" through our unity with God, then the old concepts of heaven and hell, God and man, good and evil, will pass away. There will no longer be questions about the meaning, purpose, or relevancy of the Bible. It will have fulfilled its purpose, its function in us—and we will be a new chapter, a new testament to its meanings.

1

Solomon's Sins

Volume 2 of Edgar Cayce's Story of the Old Testament, *Man Crowned King,* ended on the highnote of Solomon's glories.

Volume 3 begins with a study of the sins of Solomon.

A subtle lesson was underscored by Edgar Cayce in a lecture to the Bible class.

> "Solomon put heavy taxes on the people he had conquered. Later, when Rome rose to power, the Jews reaped this karma by having to pay tribute to Rome. It seems that Solomon, being well-versed in the history of his people, would have understood the spiritual law too well to become guilty of the same persecution practiced by pharaoh."

In the first part of his reign, Solomon was faithful to the commission David had given him (1 Chronicles 28:6, 20), but in his later years he went beyond the moral and spiritual limits which constrain a good leader and stepped into those areas that make for tyranny and despotism.

Solomon was the wisest ruler in the world, yet one of the most greedy and ambitious. He was the father of many injustices and his administration fostered dangerous principles. Indeed, the weight of gold talents he received in one year—666—becomes in the Book of Revelation the symbolic "code number of the beast." (1 Kings 10:14; Revelation 13:18) This "code number" as interpreted by Edgar Cayce indicated that a person who served "the beast of self-aggrandizement, self-indulgence, self-glorification" had his days "numbered" —they were not eternal like the soul, but with a beginning and end, like a man. A man marked with the number 666 "lacks that consciousness of God and God alone directing." (281–34)

Like many leaders who are uniquely prepared and singularly outfitted for a special role and purpose, Solomon found the excitement and pleasure of material life more than he could withstand, and did not realize his own inner spiritual resources.

Edgar Cayce spoke of it to the Bible class.

"Solomon's religious ancestry and training had given him the basis for a strong life. His own request at Gibeon and his zeal in the worship of God foretold a vigorous religious career. But, though he built the temple, and in the prayer attributed to him, he expressed some of the loftiest sentiments of a man thoroughly zealous in his worship of Israel's God, his career did not fulfill his early resolves. The polytheistic worship introduced by his foreign wives into Jerusalem and his faint and ineffectual opposition to their request that their gods be shown respect led to his moral and religious deterioration."

Ultimately, as Cayce told his Bible class, Solomon lost hold upon himself, his religion, and his people, and Israel began its decline.

The whole nation lost its consciousness of God.

The ruling class—the leaders and policy makers—were rich and self-satisfied. The people were angry, frustrated, and burdened. One of the men responsible for this condition is found in the life readings—Benaiah.

BENAIAH

Benaiah figures prominently in the reigns of both Solomon and David. With Abiather, he was David's most trusted counselor, and accomplished three noteworthy exploits worthy of mention in Scripture. (2 Samuel 23:20–23; 1 Chronicles 11:22–24)

Benaiah was loyal to David and distinguished himself in military affairs. When Adonijah attempted to usurp Solomon's throne, Benaiah sided with Solomon in proclaiming him king. He put Adonijah, Joab, and Shimei to death, and succeeded to the supreme command of Solomon's army.

A Hard Taskmaster

In the life reading for a New York textile executive, Benaiah is described as the entity's most outstanding incarnation.

The reading begins:

In giving the interpretations of the records as we find them here, these are not all pretty, from some angles; but these we choose from same with the desire and purpose that this information may be a helpful experience . . .

From a particular sojourn we find the greater part of the characteristics that are manifested in the present; that in the period when the entity was the leader of, or friend to, Solomon. For the entity then was Benaiah. (3001–1)

The influence from exposure to foreign cults and royal visitors is echoed in the entity's present interest in comparative religions and philosophies, and his desire for knowledge. We find him also a "hard taskmaster," a phrase which carries the mind back to the Exodus.

Hence those inclinations or tendencies; for the individual or tendencies; for the individual would not be called a religious man, and yet there is the adherence to—or the desire for—information, knowledge, or that in which the entity interests self—in comparative religions, comparative philosophy, comparative things having to do with the mental and spiritual influences in the lives of men. Yet it also makes the entity a hard taskmaster.

The entity is very decided as to its views. Once having set itself as to its views on any proposition—whether a material, a mental condition, or about things, about people, or in any form—it takes a lot to change him! This is a real stubbornness at times, though the entity is very sure this is not true.

But if the entity will analyze itself, it will be seen that this was not only the outstanding appearance of the entity, but also from same come the greater characteristics. (3001–1)

This description of the present entity, 3001, applies equally to Benaiah.

The astrological aspects as may be indicated have little to do with this entity . . . these are far in the background to [in comparison] the characteristics of this special appearance of the entity in the earth.

Hence it makes of the entity a good leader—if there is the choosing of the spiritual import—a good director; one in whom—when the word is given—one can put one's confidence. Yet others might say just the opposite—unless in complete agreement with the ideas of the entity. But innately and deeply, the entity is honest—though isn't always honest with self; honest more with others than with self. (3001–1)

Cayce described an incarnation preceding Benaiah, also in the Holy Land, but during the time of Joshua. He then was kin to the discredited rebel Korah, and this delayed his acceptance by those in authority. Perhaps this rejection created the desire to be "remembered" which manifested in his next life.

Cayce described the urge, as the reading continued.

But ye have a soul, a mind, a body, and the Lord thy God is One! But who is thy God? Thyself, thine own interests? as they were considered during that period when ye would make of thyself one to be remembered. Well if the entity could forget what he caused his own people to bring into their experience, that led them gradually away from the way, away from the Father-God! (3001–1)

Because of the existence of certain compulsions, Cayce gave the following counsel:

But look, listen! Better stop those things of making or forcing thine own inner self to thine own self. True, thy measurement to others is the manner in which ye treat thy Maker. But thy judgments—are they in keeping with the law? that if ye cause thy brother to offend, ye are worse than the infidel?

Let that which was the directing force in the law keep thy ways, thy directions, and ye will find ye will come into a closer, better understanding of the purposes of life, and find greater joy in same. (3001–1)

The great material glories of Solomon's reign were built upon a weak foundation of heavy taxation and forced labor, over which this entity had been "a hard taskmaster." The charge that Solomon was "a greedy and relentless autocrat," whose despotism created feelings of social injustice and class hatred, is echoed in the following.

Just as the desire for knowledge has remained with Mr. 3001 since the days of Solomon, so, too, have the anguished cries of the people.

. . . the entity was in that land and during the period when Solomon, the son of David, was king of Israel; when the entity, as Benaiah, was raised to one of authority, one of power, and yet one who brought to himself—while in the material plane gratifying experiences, and wonderments in the mental —those judgments that must be corrected in the present.

Be well if the entity would analyze and study especially the life of that leader of the peoples, as to how servitude was brought about, as to how the various groups—as to classes—became a part of the experience through much of the activity of the entity in that period; and the lack of the due consideration or stress put upon man's relationship to Creative Forces in that experience. (3001–1)

The reading contains a yardstick for Mr. 3001 to measure his mental and spiritual growth. Perhaps this advice could be applied equally well to Solomon.

> What gains the man if he gains the whole world and loses his own soul? or what can the man give in exchange for his soul? For, the purpose of the manifestation of individuality in the earth is to be to the glory of God, not to the gratifying of self, nor of that ego, nor to be well-spoken of. To be well-spoken of is beautiful, but is this of self or to the glory of the Creative Force? (3001–1)

CORONATION AND REBELLION

And Solomon slept with his fathers, and they buried him in the city of David; and Rehoboam his son reigned in his stead. (2 Chronicles 9: 31)

The lack of sensitivity to the needs of the people shown in Solomon and Benaiah was passed on to Solomon's son and successor, Rehoboam—and resulted in the tragedy of rebellion, secession, and civil war.

The assembly for Rehoboam's coronation was at Shechem, the one sacred, historic city within the province of the ten tribes. Before the coronation, the assembly requested reforms in Solomon's policies. The old men, who had seen the evils of Solomon's course, advised Rehoboam to yield to the people; but the young princes, accustomed to the pleasures of a brilliant court, were not willing to modify a policy that yielded to them such large privileges. The reforms would reduce the royal exchequer and its power to continue the magnificence of the court.

Apparently Rehoboam had no spiritual understanding, Cayce told his Bible class. Rehoboam took advantage of his material power, but never considered the privilege he had of serving the people in a spiritual sense.

The young princes urged Rehoboam to increase the revenues, and Rehoboam consented. The counsel was callous and selfish:

> *Thus shall you speak to the people who have said to you, Your father made our yoke heavy, but make you it lighter for us; Thus shall you answer them, My little finger is thicker than my father's thumb. And now whereas my father laid a heavy yoke on you, I will add to your yoke . . . (1 Kings 12:10)*

The advice of the young princes gave rise to this revealing interpretation in the readings.

> Things that are of the spirit must arise from the spiritual promptings; things that are material arise from the material promptings. What seek ye? Remember, my children, those examples shown thee. What spoke the Lord? Know ye not that where thy burdens have been as those of the finger, they shall become as thick as the thigh? Know ye not that those that seek material things must in all things pay the price of same? (254–85)

The world affairs readings carefully delineate the eternal and unchanging causes of all disturbance between men. Hostilities and animosities between men stem from one basic and fundamental principle: Man forgets God and, in the forgetting, loses sight of the fact that he is his brother's keeper.

In Solomon's reign, many one-sided advantages accrued to the royal house. Under Solomon's hand, with "hard taskmasters" such as Benaiah, the unified kingdom of David began to dissolve from within. Even in Solomon's lifetime, Jeroboam, who was later to play such a commanding role in the impending revolution, "lifted up his hand" in revolt. (1 Kings 11:26)

> Yes, we have . . . those problems which have brought about the upheavals and the wars, the distrust, the jealousy, the hate existing today. These are the result of man's forgetting God, and that which truly represents man's sincere attempt to worship, honor, and glorify a living God.
>
> For this may only be done in the manner in which individuals, states, nations, treat their fellow man. For, as ye do unto others, ye do to thy Maker. And when those activities are such as to dishonor thy fellow man, ye dishonor thy God—and it brings all of those forms of disturbance that exist in the world today. (3976-28)

One of the central teachings in Genesis is that we are our brother's keeper. The world affairs discourses stress this fact.

The following interprets its import. Revolution is the leveler. Only love can prevent it.

> . . . just as indicated . . . we ARE our brother's keeper.
>
> Then if those in position to give of their means, their wealth, their education, their position, DO NOT take these things into consideration, there must be that leveling that will come.
>
> For unless these are considered, there must eventually become a revolution . . . and there will be a dividing of the sections as one against another. For these are the leveling means and manners to which men resort

when there is the plenty in SOME areas and a lack of the sustenance in the life of others.

These are the manners in which such things as crime, riots, and every nature of disturbance arise—in that those who are in authority are not considering every level, every phase of human activity and human experience . . .

Then those who are in power must know that they ARE their brother's keeper, and give expression to that which has been indicated in "Thou shalt love the Lord thy God with all thy heart and mind and body, and thy neighbor as thyself." . . .

But when there becomes class or mass distinction between this or that group, this or that party, this or that faction, then it becomes a class rather than "thy neighbor as thyself."

For all stand as ONE before Him. For the Lord is NOT a respecter of persons, and these things CANNOT long exist. (3976–19)

Isaiah forecasted social revolution, based on the same principle:

The foot shall tread it down, even the feet of the poor and the steps of the needy. (Isaiah 26:6)

For those who are hungry care not as to the source of strength or power, until there is the fulfilling of that desired.

Unless there is, then, a more universal oneness of purpose on the part of all, this will one day bring . . . revolution! (3976–24)

An earlier reading in the same series repeats the warning.

And there CANNOT be one measuring stick for the laborer in the field and the man behind the counter, and another for the man behind the money changers. ALL are equal —not only under the material law but under the SPIRITUAL.

And HIS laws, HIS will, will not come to naught!

Though there may come those periods when there will be great stress, as brother rises against brother, as group or sect or race rises against race—yet the leveling must come. (3976-18)

The laws are not new. The results are not new. The pattern remains unchanged. From the beginning, man has been instructed to love. Although the command to "love your neighbor as yourself" is considered new, it is one which man has had from the start. According to John (1 John 3:11), it is just another way of saying "We are our brother's keeper." The law, which Israel had before them always was simply stated, reaffirmed, and amplified by Jesus.

Rehoboam took the self-serving advice of his young counselors, which resulted in the rebellion of the ten tribes and the beginning of a history of civil war, heartaches, suffering, tragedy, and the ultimate degeneration and effacement of both kingdoms.

TO YOUR TENTS, O ISRAEL!

Divine revelation is an eternal process and, like the Creation, still continues. The Bible is a mirror of the processes of growth and change, and bears witness to man's progressive discovery of the truth.

Thus we discover that *all time* is *one time,* and that the Bible contains patterns that emerge in our own lives.

The material aspects of Solomon's reign were the

most transient part of his glory, yet the most blinding to the carnal mind. And it is still the same today. The lust for material things blinded his successors and kept them from seeing their true spiritual purpose. Thus, in the cycle following Solomon, there was a steady rise in the prophetic voice with its insistence on repentance, preparation, and purity.

The changes which took place after Solomon's passing are part of the process of spiritualization. The disturbances following Solomon were the preface to a new order and understanding among men, completed in the master Jesus who obtained Christ-consciousness and fulfilled the Biblical pattern in its entirety.

As in Solomon's day the "old order" had to pass away for new forms and consciousness to emerge. Cayce told his contemporaries in a world affairs reading:

> It is also understood, comprehended by some, that a new order of conditions is to arise; that there must be many a purging in high places as well as low; that there must be the greater consideration of each individual, each soul being his brother's keeper.
>
> There will come then about those circumstances in the political, the economic and the whole relationships where there will be a leveling—or a greater comprehension of this need . . . For His ways will carry through. For as He gave, "Though the heavens and the earth may pass away, My word will NOT pass away." (3976–18)

All the promises in the Bible are conditional. There is an "if" clause attached to every one, including those to Solomon.

However, because Solomon had so blatantly failed to honor his part of the covenant, changes became necessary that prove "God is not mocked" and that His words are words of power and truth.

The secession of the ten tribes was according to God's judgment. It was the way through which the "old order" would be changed, the high brought low, and the low exalted. Each new age in the evolution of spiritual consciousness is prefaced by the breaking up of conditions which are blocks and barriers to the light. Conditions around us are ever working toward the fulfillment of God's word.

When Rehoboam would not listen to the people, they answered the king, saying:

"We have no portion in David, neither have we inheritance in the son of Jesse, to your tents, O Israel!" (1 Kings 12:16-20)

The rebellion marks the beginning of the final phase in the Old Testament story.

With the loss of the ten tribes, the royal tribe of Judah would be made weak, and in its weakness would regain its true strength—by its need for God.

The ten tribes, forming now a separate and independent kingdom, would constitute a "new order" with new opportunities.

The prophet Abijah had foreseen Jeroboam as the man with the necessary qualifications to lead the new kingdom. To Abijah, and others of the ten tribes, Jeroboam was the logical choice because, as the young rebel who had lifted up his hand against Solomon, he possessed, if nothing else, the courage of his convictions.

A leader was present whom the people felt could meet their needs. This is ever true, and a fulfillment of a spiritual law.

And then there should be, there WILL be those rising to power that are able to meet the needs. For none are in power but that have been given the opportunity by the will of the Father—from which all power emanates.

Hence those will be leveled with the purpose, "My word shall NOT fail!" (3976–18)

2

Jeroboam, King of Israel

---

*The man Jeroboam was a mighty man of val-
our (1 Kings 11:28)*

Jeroboam was promised as sure a house as David's, but the promise was conditional. His house would
be stable only "if" he walked in the ways of God.
(1 Kings 11:38)

No doubt Jeroboam had been conditioned and
prepared through experiences in past lives for the opportunities and responsibilities of his new career. He
was put in a unique position. Like Saul he was the
standard bearer in a new age. He was a model for
the new kingdom. Things would be made better or
worse according to his choices.

Jeroboam was given his chance because he answered to the needs of the people. There was an authenticity to his call which made it divine. He felt the
injustice and unrest, thus the spirit of God's purposes
could work through him, magnifying the leadership
qualities he possessed.

Many are called, but few have chosen, Cayce
once told the Bible class. Not *are* chosen, but *have*
chosen—for the call comes to every soul. What is a
"call"? A practical and working definition is suggested
in an early world affairs reading. Basically, it is the

willingness of an entity to choose to be used "as an instrument of good for the saving of the good in human principles."—A call to which all can harken and apply in every phase and all relationships of daily living.

> First the choosing of those who would give self in holy communion with this one purpose and, making self right with God, choose to be used as an *instrument* of good for the saving of the good in human principles; for, as is seen, as has been given, the world awaits the coming of those who will proclaim the day of freedom from the bonds of those who would rule, either through prestige or through political influence, see? Then ones so chosen by their fitness—as will come through such communion—will be the first to begin. (3976-4)

The readings indicate we are "chosen" if we choose. We have a "call" if we but listen. The Spirit bids all to follow, and the closer we draw to the Source the more we will be able to manifest its attributes—psychic and spiritual forces. The Cayce readings make it clearly evident, whether we are conscious of the fact or not, that we can and are, by our moods, attitudes and convictions, creating the spiritual, mental and physical environment of our worlds.

By harmonious co-operation with the divine, our souls are opened by the Spirit which activates and magnifies those talents and abilities within, which will enable us to fulfill our purpose. By following these creative impulses, we develop skills, abilities, and understandings which lead us into greater spheres of activity and responsibility. In future incarnations we are drawn to situations where we will have the opportunity to use that which we have developed.

Like Jeroboam, we will all have the opportunity to be standard bearers. But unlike Jeroboam, pray that we may resist the temptations that make us fall and pervert the purpose of our call.

> Let him that is weak of mind or heart not take the handle, for he that ploweth and looketh back is worse than the infidel. 3976–4)

JEROBOAM'S FALL

> In [this entity] there is seen the abilities of the use of power and of principle, yet that inner self must be made over again, as it were, in that oneness of the purpose as has often been set in self . . . for before each there is set a way, and in that way is set a light. Veer not from same! (3976–4)

All power or authority comes from God. Because Jeroboam had been responsive to the needs of his brothers, he was raised to authority. However, "few does power not destroy." (3976–13) Once in power Jeroboam determined to retain his position no matter what the cost.

His guile is shown immediately. When Rehoboam returned to Jerusalem and was crowned king over Judah, he assembled his men of war to fight against Israel. However, the prophet Shemaiah spoke out against his intentions, saying that the division of the tribes was God's work and that the tribe of Judah should not wage war against its brothers. (1 Kings 12: 22–24)

Rehoboam obeyed the prophet and disbanded his men.

By accepting God's word, Rehoboam had unconsciously provided a non-violent solution to the disunity. The Israelites still had strong mental, emotional and spiritual ties with Jerusalem, especially the temple. They desired to return to the city to worship. Perhaps in this desire the differences could have been settled or overcome, and the nation united again, if Jeroboam hadn't interfered. Jeroboam saw, in the desire of his people to return to Jerusalem to worship, a strong threat to his independent authority. Rather than lead the people back to worship, and risk losing his temporal crown, Jeroboam instituted worship of the golden calf and built altars for the burning of "the sandalwoods of Egypt." (See 274–10)

> *And Jeroboam said in his heart, Now the kingdom will return to the house of David; If this people go up to do sacrifices at the house of the Lord in Jerusalem, then shall the heart of this people turn again to their lord, even to Rehoboam king of Judah, and they shall kill me . . . So the king took counsel, and made two calves of gold, and said to all Israel, It is too much for you to go up to Jerusalem; behold your gods, Oh Israel, who brought you up out of the land of Egypt. (1 Kings 12:26–28)*

Cayce gave his analysis of this section of the Book of Kings to the Bible class:

> "Jeroboam may have started with a good purpose, but it didn't last long. He used politics to get power. He took advantage of the people's unrest and made himself popular. In other words, Jeroboam was the lesser of two evils. They were in that consciousness now that a king was necessary to them, and Rehoboam had failed."

The readings commented on two sources of Jeroboam's corruption. First, his counselors.

> Look upon those that were called into service as was Saul, the son of Kish; as was

Jeroboam, the son of Nebat. These came by
the divine call from out of their brethren and
were endowed with that which would make
for such a manifestation as had not before
been seen in the earth. Yet counselors of
these made them but laughingstocks to the
nations roundabout. (254–85)

Second the ever-present evil of self-indulgence.
This practice may have started during Jeroboam's exile
in Egypt. (1 Kings 11:39)

What did Jeroboam, that he made the
children of Israel to sin, but to offer rather
the sandalwoods of the nations or the Egyp-
tians that made for the arousing of the passions in man for the gratifications of the
seeking for the activities that would satisfy
his own indulgence, rather than the offering
of those things that would make for the
glory of the Lord's entrance into the activities of the individual! (274–10)

The world affairs readings contain the statement:
that when "selfishness is the prompting attitude"; turmoils and strife follow as a natural effect. (3976–17)
Another reading states:

Rather does man—by his compliance with
the divine law—bring order out of chaos;
or by his *disregard of* the associations and
laws of divine influence, brings chaos and
destructive forces into his experience. (416–
7)

The spirit of selfishness characterizes Jeroboam as
king, and this vibration was perpetuated in all the
leaders who followed him, creating in their wake a
national history filled with regicide, revolution, count-

er-revolution, pogroms, and persecution, ceasing only with their effacement through conquest and captivity by a foreign power.

Many were the kings who were "valiant in the ways of the earth," but, as Jeremiah states, knew little of the ways of the Spirit. (Jeremiah 9:3) Men such as Omri and Baasha were brilliant military leaders, and others like Jeroboam and Ahab were gifted political strategists who "did right" in terms of self-preservation and increasing their power base. They did that which seemed right at the moment (Romans 6:21), and often their efforts were successful for a short time, but seldom for more than a generation. The end result was death, decline, and change. With all its efforts toward self-preservation, Israel could not save itself.

A recurrent refrain echoes through all the dynasties of Israel. All the nineteen kings "walked in the sins of Jeroboam" and "made Israel to sin."

Jeroboam was another Saul, but no David rose up after him to offset his influence. The sin was violation of the first commandment.

> For, the first law that has been given to man from the beginning is: "Thou shalt have no other gods before me." And when man has faltered, has altered . . . that command that has come to man throughout the ages, then there arises that which creates those things that are the fruits of the evil influences that are in the earth. Such as: hate, jealousy, avarice, and the like. These make for the creating of those conditions in all walks of life for power, for position, for the love of money and that it will bring in its associations in the lives of individuals . . . For, with that command has come ever that to which mankind may expect to find himself reduced when he has forgotten that which is

his *first* duty, and the second which is likened unto it: "Thou shalt love thy neighbor as thyself."

Then, this condition has been the experience in the greater portion of the whole nation, the whole world. For that is the experience of the individual that makes for the creating in his environs, his surrounding, of that which breeds strife, that which breeds hate, that which breeds malice, that which breeds selfishness. (3976–14)

JEROBOAM AND THE MAN OF GOD
(1 Kings 13)

Sometime after his eighth month as king, Jeroboam was burning incense at his altar when he was approached by a prophet who spoke out against him.

The man of God had come from Judah to warn Jeroboam that unless he changed his inner purpose, men's bones would eventually be burnt from his altar. Jeroboam was beginning to lead the children of Israel astray, and God was trying to warn him.

Jeroboam was incensed at the prophet and put up his hand (perhaps the same one he lifted against Solomon) to strike the man of God, and as he did, the arm withered. The angry king instantly became fearful, and implored the prophet to heal his hand.

Cayce made a wise observation, as he lectured on this episode:

"Notice that Jeroboam did not entreat his own god, but asked the man of God to intreat *his* god. If he had asked for the strength to change his heart, to do the right, no doubt the future would have been entirely different. He only asked for his hand to be restored—apparently so he could carry on his evil doing in the same way he started."

21

A similar note is struck in a world affairs reading:

> Let each and every soul call on not their
> god but the One God! (3976–26)

When people sought physical help, often the readings asked why the individual wanted to be healed. All illness comes from sin (misapplication of spiritual laws), the readings stressed. If the purpose for the healing was only to enable the entity to carry on in the same life-style that had brought on the affliction, it could be better for the person to suffer until he had a change of heart and learned the lesson of his pain.

A reading on healing prayer tells us:

> And if thy life is disturbed, if thy heart
> is sad, if thy body is racked with pain, it is
> thine bungling of the laws that are as uni-
> versal as Life itself. (281–27)

Life is of God, and only by seeking God can we come to know the purpose for Life. "Those He loves, He chastens and purges," the reading states, that we may produce fruit worthy of our Creator.

The instant healing did not change Jeroboam. He continued to "bungle" his opportunity to be a spiritual leader. Perhaps if he had not been healed so readily, he would have remained in awe and fear of the Lord, and the course of history would have been changed.

Although this chapter may seen like an interlude in the general context of the story, it contains important lessons, to which the Cayce readings add an additional richness.

The story does not end with Jeroboam, but leaves him standing at the altar and follows the man of God on his way home.

Jeroboam implored the prophet to come to his home to eat with him, and so he could give him presents. The prophet replied emphatically:

"If you give me half your house, I will not go home with you, For so it was charged me by the word of the Lord, saying, Eat no bread and drink no water, nor return again by the way you came." (1Kings 13:8–9)

The prophet headed home by a different route, but his journey was interrupted by another prophet, an old man, who had heard what the man of God had done. The old prophet invited the younger man to his home for food and drink, but the prophet refused. The old prophet then responded that "an angel spoke to me by the word of the Lord" to invite him to bread and water at his home.

The young man accepted, and dined with the old prophet. Suddenly, during the meal, the old prophet stood up and cried out, "Because you have disobeyed the word of the Lord and have not kept the commandment he commanded you, your corpse shall not rest in the sepulchre of your fathers."

The two men finished their meal. On the way back to Beth-el, the prophet was attacked by a lion and slain.

In the Cayce library there are several remarkable readings for individuals with great psychic abilities. Among the most interesting is one given for a six-year-old Rhode Island child. The boy was told that in a previous incarnation he had been the man of God who warned Jeroboam and in a succeeding incarnation had been the great psychic whose conversation is told in Acts 8:5–23.

Although the story of the two prophets is one of the most unusual and enigmatic in the whole Old Testament, with meanings that are not easily reached, perhaps this reading and Edgar Cayce's commentary will add new insights.

The reading began:

Yes, we have the records here of that entity now known as or called [4087].

As we find, there are great possibilities but there are also great problems to be met with the training and the direction for this entity through the formative years.

For as we find this entity has more than once been among those who were gifted with what is sometimes called second sight, or the super-activity of the third eye. Whenever there is the opening, then, of the lyden [Leydig] center and the kundaline forces from along the pineal, we find that there are visions of things to come, of things that are happening.

Yet in the use of these through some experiences, as we will find, the entity is in the present meeting itself. For the entity was the prophet who warned Jereboam. Read it! You will see why he is not to listen at all of those who may counsel him as to the manner in which he is to use the abilities that have been and are a portion of the entity's experience; but to trust in Him who is the way. (4087–1)

The old prophet's ability to change the young man's mind about God's message is an indication of a larger weakness in the entity that is being met and must be learned in the present—to be true to his own inner guidance and counsel, and not to be led astray by others, no matter how well-intentioned.

Cayce's commentary to the Bible class could be included as an interpretation of the reading:

"The other man was also a prophet, or had been. How do you suppose he fooled the man of God? So often, even the best of us are fooled by flattery. The old prophet didn't say God had spoken to him, but an angel. Perhaps it was a fallen angel. At any rate, the man of God listened to what another had to say, rather than remaining true to what he had been told himself.

"No matter what someone's else's command is, or how conflicting it may be with ours, it is up to us to carry out OUR orders. This old prophet was a channel for evil, perhaps unintentionally, just as the serpent was for Eve when it said, 'Ye shall not surely die.'

"The same old prophet who led him astray became the channel for the message of doom.

"The old prophet's gesture of repentance was seeing that the man of God received a prophet's burial. He recognized his part in the man's fall from grace, and was sorry. A man of God was very rare in those days, and he wanted some congenial company—someone who could talk his language, as it were.

"This demonstrates how necessary it is for us to watch our every move, to be sure that our prompting is of the very highest source; else we, too, may lead someone astray."

The reading describes how the entity turned aside:

. . . the entity was the prophet of Judah who was sent to Jeroboam to warn him, and who brought about the withering of the hand,

and also the healing of same; *yet turned aside when faced with that in which the mind said, "A more excellent way."*

The reading continues, with valuable counsel to the parents:

There are no short cuts. What God hath commanded is true. For the law of the Lord is perfect and it converteth the soul.

Here the parents have a real, real obligation. They have a real, real opportunity. So live in self that thine own lives may be an example to this entity through its formative years. So teach, not let it be given to someone else—so teach for it is thy responsibility, not the priest's, not a teacher's, *not* a minister's responsibility, but thine. Don't put it off. Don't neglect, or else ye will meet self again.

In the training let it first begin with self, as with the entity [4087]. Joseph he should be called. Let the training begin with that indicated in Exodus 19:5—"If thou will harken to the voice, He hath a special work, a special mission for thee—but thou must harken to the voice within, that ye present thy body as a living sacrifice, holy and acceptable unto Him, which is a reasonable service." For they who have been called, who have been ordained to be messengers have the greater responsibility; not as a saint— for there is more joy in heaven over one sinner than ninety and nine who are so-called saints, or those who are themselves satisfied with that they do.

Then study that interpreted in Romans. Ye will find it is not from somewhere else, not from out of the blue, not from overseas, not from before the altar. For thy body is indeed the temple and there he may indeed meet his Maker. There indeed may he meet himself. There indeed may he open the door of his own consciousness so that the Master may walk and talk with him.

Do not discourage, do not encourage the visions—until the first lessons are learned.

Then there will be the needs that *thou,* as well as others, take heed to the warnings this entity may be sent to give. (4087–1) (Italics added)

THE KINGDOM OF JUDAH

If the history of the kingdom of Israel (the ten tribes) reflects the inevitable consequences of selfishness, the kingdom of Judah, while sharing many features in common, reveals the fruits of spiritualization. Both kingdoms warred with each other, knew bitter internal strife, followed false gods, and were conquered and made captives by foreign nations. But the kingdom of Israel became "lost" while the kingdom of Judah preserved its identity and fulfilled its purpose for being in the earth. Man must remember *who* he is, and complete *his* purpose—which is to be *one* with God.

If Cayce's premise is correct and the Bible is the story of man, and its history contains the pattern or process of his complete unfoldment, a meaning must be assigned to the disappearance of all but one of the twelve tribes. Ten are "lost," swept from the stage of the apocalyptic drama; and Benjamin, the only other royal tribe, is absorbed by Judah and gradually loses its separate identity. Of all the great numbers in Israel, only Judah remains, and that is reduced to a remnant. And it is those few who, at the end, complete the pattern.

God is a consuming fire, a purifier, purging the

drosses in man, cleansing the soul from all that separates it from Him. Judah was purified by Fire which, according to Isaiah, was "the light of Israel," and its flame was "his Holy One." (Isaiah 10:17) "Behold," the prophet writes, "I have refined you, but not with silver; I have purified you in the furnace of affliction." (Isaiah 48:10)

Jesus, who was the crown of Judah, "learned obedience through the things he suffered." (Hebrews 5:8; 262-56, 262-82)

Judah passed through "the furnace of affliction" and came out of captivity in Babylon with "a will to mind the things of God."

Perhaps this pattern of rejection and selectivity, as once large numbers are consistently worked down and reduced to a handful, and then to one, should emphasize to man how much he has filled his body, mind, and soul with a clutter that prevents him from seeing the purity he should treasure most highly; and how much the flame of the "Holy One" has to burn away before that vision is gained.

A reading tells us:

> . . . what is the will of the Father? That no soul should perish! And *all* will be—all *are* —tried so as by fire. The fires of nature are what? Self-indulgence, self-glorification. (3976-23)

The Story Begins

During the first eighty-five years of the new kingdom, Israel was rent with revolution and regicide. During most of the same period, the kingdom of Judah experienced continued stability and growth.

Solomon's worship of "earthly forces" (900-428) had made its deteriorating effect upon the national consciousness and had begun a cycle of decline. However, two morally and spiritually responsible kings, and their prophets, working with and through a believing populace, were able to "keep the spirit alive" and reverse the downward trend.

The kingdom of Israel had nineteen kings, representing four dynasties. With the exception of Ahab, whose wife Jezebel tried to forcibly implant Baal worship as the state religion, each king practiced a form of religious toleration, which allowed a multiplicity of cults to flourish. As Israel became populated with an astonishing variety of "gods," its spiritual life became hopelessly fragmented, and deterioration became inevitable. The nation lacked a loyalty focus for the highest aspirations of its people.

But Judah possessed the temple and the tradition that it was the royal and chosen tribe of God. It had a point of unity, a spiritual focus for binding all the mental, spiritual, and emotional energies of the people. Whereas Jeroboam could not risk a spiritual revival for fear of losing his hold upon the people, Judah could not afford to be without one. Their only hope as a "chosen" people was to lose themselves in a wholehearted search for God's will. Thus, as the children of Judah strove to fulfill the "if" clause in their covenant, we find them much more creative, imaginative, inventive, and bold in their worship, and in the application of their faith in many challenging situations, with astonishing—but predictable and promised—results.

THE DOWNWARD KINGS

Rehoboam and Abijah

Rehoboam reigned seventeen years and followed the ways of Solomon and not David. In Rehoboam's fifth year as king, the children of Judah had drifted so far from their understanding of God that they lost His protection. Jerusalem was invaded and the royal palace was sacked. Just twenty years after its dedication, the temple was desecrated. The prophet Shemaiah informed the king and his princes that the destruction was the result of their forsaking God.

Abijah followed Rehoboam, and ruled three years. "He walked in all the sins of his father, and his heart was not perfect . . . like the heart of David." (1 Kings 15:3)

Although Rehoboam repented sufficiently after Shemaiah's rebuke to turn away "the wrath of God" (2 Chronicles 12:12), and Abijah had enough faith to march against Jeroboam when outnumbered two-to-one (2 Chronicles 13:3), neither monarch could offset Judah's rapid decline. All Solomon's pomp and glory withered instantly.

The condition was neither karmic nor predestined. One man whose "heart was perfect" could have offset the trend. Judah needed not another Solomon but a David.

One reading asked:

Why then the turmoil in the world today? (3976–24)

The answer was basic:

They have forgotten God! Not that it is merely a karmic condition of a nation, of a people; for, know ye not that the prayer of one man saved a city? (3976–24)

The solution is unchanging, with the same answer found both in the Bible and the readings.

Q–3. What can we do to counteract such serious [future trouble]?
A–3. Make known the trouble—WHERE IT LIES; THAT THEY WHO HAVE FORGOTTEN GOD MUST RIGHT ABOUT FACE! (3976–26)

Asa and Jehoshaphat

. . . though in hardships, though in trials,
though in tribulation, there was found by
the entity that those who seek the Lord
while He may be found—and have a work-
able knowledge of His desires toward men—
may have that as is builded-in in a material
position, whether it be fame, fortune, social,
or what . . . (1733–2)

The downward trend was reversed by Asa, who
listened to his prophets and "remembered" God.

The prophet Azariah went out and challenged
Asa at the beginning of his reign with this warning:

*"Hear me Asa, the Lord is with you for ever and
ever; if you seek Him, He will be found by you;
but if you forsake Him, he will forsake you.*
(2 Chronicles 15:2)

Cayce spoke briefly but wisely on this counsel to the
Bible class.

"The prophet assured Asa that the Lord
would be with him as long as he sought
God, but if he forsook God then God would
forsake him. This truth is constantly before
us. As Jesus said, we are gods in the making." [John 10:34]

Rehoboam and Abijah were intent upon emulat-
ing Solomon, while Asa looked back to David. Asa
"did right in the sight of the Lord, as did David his
father." (1 Kings 15:11) The new king's heart "was

perfect with the Lord his God all his days." (1 Kings 15:5)

He inherited great problems, but was able to solve most of them by setting an example and drawing the people back to a greater reliance or dependence upon the spirit.

"And he said to Judah, Come, let us pray before the Lord God of our Fathers." (2 Chronicles 14:4)

Thus we find in a world affairs readings that this is a good practice for any nation.

Yet, as we find, if there is the turning of every man and woman to the thought of God, then we may solve every problem. For it is not by mere thought, not by any activity other than the moving force [of God] within each entity, each body; and when more of patience, more tolerance, more thought of others is advanced and kept in the heart of the individual, this lends that power, that influence, that force for good.

Ye are to have turmoils, ye are to have strifes . . . [How to] meet same? Only that each soul turn not to self alone and cry for strength, but that each soul LIVE in such a manner that there may be the awakening to the needs, the purposes, the causes for the nation coming into existence! (3976–24)

Asa began strengthening his people by uprooting the pagan practices which had led Judah away from the spiritual ideals of David.

. . . no government, no nation, no state, no city, no family—yes, no individual—is stronger than the weakest habit; the destructive forces that may in any way or manner at any time undermine if they are self-purposing.

But if the ideas and the ideals are rather that each should be, each WILL be, each purposing to be, a channel for presenting brotherly love, kindness, patience, long-suffering, just being kind . . . we will find more and more that there will be drawn the greater dawn of EVERY FORM of helpfulness, hopefulness, in the experience of an individual, a family, a state, a city, a nation.

Not that there may not be those things that have been so well presented as in the days before the flood; they were married, given in marriage; there were the reckless, there were the saints. As in those days before the end may come, these may be ever JUST the same.

But man being a creative nature, man being endowed with divinity within self, may work that to his own undoing or to his own glory in the Father, the Son and the Holy Spirit that worketh in and through those according to that purposed in their hearts. (3976–17)

Opposition to Asa's reforms must have been strong and fierce.

Pagan worship had made its inroads even into the royal family. The queen mother worshiped foreign cults and must have influenced Asa's father, Abijah, in the dangerous course he followed as king. In spite of her son's reforms, Maachah continued in the pagan cult until Asa was forced to depose her.

The unseating of Asa's mother (2 Chronicles 15: 16) suggested to Cayce that Asa's spiritual commitment superseded the natural ties of flesh and blood

—or, as Jesus said, "Who is my mother, my father or brother? He who does the will of God." (Matthew 12; Mark 3)

The episode drew out a commentary on human nature for the Bible class.

> "Why would Asa be a good king, whereas Abijah, his father [2 Chronicles 14:1], had been an evil one. Asa took advantage of the opportunity to study the law and tried to fulfill it. Abijah sought only his own personal interests.
>
> "Asa paid attention to the teachers, and those who on certain days read the law. Others paid no attention. Human nature hasn't changed one whit since Adam! Will it have to change? What is human nature? When Jesus was in the garden and betrayed, He reminded his disciples, 'I have the power to call a legion of angels.' Certainly it was very much against human nature not to do it. He had the ability to come down from the cross, even in the hour of suffering. Certainly He could have done that, when He had the power to raise himself from the grave. But He deliberately allowed His body to die. That is a change in human nature. The natural thing would have been self-preservation. Yes, we must change human nature. We must eventually reach the place where we say, as Jesus, 'I'll pay it all now, and won't have to go through this anymore.'
>
> "Asa went against human nature when he took his mother from the throne because of her idols."

However, as Cayce observed, Asa's "human nature" was not completely overcome.

"But he did not destroy the places for idol worship that had been established by Solomon. Practically on every hill Solomon had allowed high places to be built to the various household gods worshiped by his wives. Asa didn't remove those places. He knew he could not afford to bring on his head the condemnation from all those groups of people. This was a very human reaction. Perhaps if he had undertaken to destroy those high places, he would have received divine help just as the many other leaders had done in the past. Asa missed that opportunity of becoming a great power for good. He might have changed the whole Biblical history. As it is, he receives honorable mention due to the fact that he tried to do that which was right in his own household."

Asa was put to the test in another arena. In the bold and creative traditions of the past, he went to war against "a million Ethiopians" with a handful of men. (2 Chronicles 14)

It is, then, still the challenge to each country, to each nation—that while there is, to be sure, the natural instinct or purpose of self-preservation, it is to be less and less of self and more and more for that which was from the beginning. (3976-23)

From the beginning, the people had been promised that, if their small numbers were in harmony with God's purposes, they would never be intimidated by larger forces.

For as has been said of old, If the Lord be with *one* he shall put ten *thousand* to flight. (262-96)

The Lord is thy strength and thy redeemer
... And they that keep His ways need not
fear. For harm of a *destructive* nature *cannot* come nigh to those that love Him. (262–
98)

Or,

For, as it has been given, "Yea, though there
be only ten just men, they may save the city;
they may save the nation; they may save
the world." (3976–14)

Therefore, Asa prayed:

*Thou art our Lord, thou art the help of thy peo-
ple; and when thou dost deliver a great army in
the hands of a small force, then all the inhabi-
tants of the earth shall know it is good to rely
on thee. (2 Chronicles 14:11)* *

Asa was victorious and this army was the only
one he had to face until the thirty-fifth year of his
reign, when Baasha, the "wicked," came up against
him. (1 Kings 15) Baasha was the third king of
Israel. He had come to the throne through a military
coup and by murdering Nadab, Jeroboam's son. Baasha
was so wicked that he was not even buried, after ruling twenty-four years. (1 Kings 16)

Cayce's comments about Baasha indicate the spiritual climate among the ten tribes which made a dramatic contrast to the reign of Asa which, for the most
part, was contemporaneous.

"The most horrible thing that could be
imagined at that time (and possibly in the
present) was for anyone not to have a de-

---

*Lamsa translation.

cent burial. From the very fact that Abraham had prepared the special burying place for his family, it had become a matter of principle among the Israelites. Baasha and his house had gotten so far away from the worship of the one true God that even such a material consideration as this was not to be shown. They were not to have a monument to their memory. No descendant could be proud of what they had done. They were to be outcasts, not counted worthy to be buried in consecrated ground. This shows how far they had gotten away from the idea of oneness.

Baasha's intrusion against Judah was unsuccessful. Asa entered into a league with the king of Damascus, which forced Baasha to withdraw. However, to finance this alliance, Asa took gold and silver from the temple treasury.

Although the solution was bloodless and politically successful, Asa was rebuked by his prophet Hanan for relying upon "an arm of flesh" and not keeping his heart "perfect in his worship." Hanan scorned Asa for not seeking to understand "all God's wonders" for "the Lord will fight for you." (2 Chronicles 16)

All that we can ever know of God is within us, the readings state, and our knowledge is gained only by application of the things we already know. They grow as we use them. No individual can ever realize his own potential until he learns to trust wholly in God. We all possess souls, and the soul is "the image of God." What is meant by "His Spirit will work through us?" The full implication is given in Jesus' words, "Greater things than these, ye shall do!" (John 14:12)

Asa was in a position where he could again demonstrate the power and protection of God, if he trusted God against Baasha as he had against "the million

Ethiopians." Why he didn't we don't know. It's not given in the record.

Asa was in a commanding position to give an example to his people and to posterity. His faith in the past had been seasoned with prosperity, victory, and blessings. Yet Asa encountered a situation with Baasha where he failed to apply his spiritual insights. The fact that he outwardly depleted the temple treasury to finance his alliance symbolizes the inward fact that he robbed his own soul (his temple) of a vital experience he could have known through the application of his faith.

All the "good" kings of Judah, until Jesus, followed a similar pattern. In certain areas they showed remarkable faith and spiritual development, applying these truths for the benefit of their nation. Yet in other areas they fell short. When the weaknesses of their "human nature" dictated their policies, and not the strength of their souls, their efforts produced short-term and immediate benefits, but to future generations brought bitter fruit.

We are all "kings," and too often our own choices (in terms of the soul) are not best in the long development, although they may be instantly gratifying to the ego and the carnal sense.

Whenever a king made a bad decision (from the spiritual point of view) there was always a prophet to remind him.

GOOD KING JEHOSHAPHAT

Jehoshaphat continued the spiritual and religious reforms of his father, Asa, and "walked in the first ways of David." (2 Chronicles 17:4) The "first ways," Cayce told his Bible class, refers to the spiritual ideals of David which not all David's ancestors followed. He "prayed to the Lord God" and kept all his commandments and statutes. (v. 4) His "heart was strengthened in the ways of the Lord" and he uprooted the altars and high places in Judah. (v. 6) Jehoshaphat took advantage of the peace he inherited from his father and continued strengthening his kingdom with walls, fortifications, and a large standing army. Thus peace, prosperity, and security continued in Judah.

"The Lord God established the kingdom in his hand" (v. 5) and "Jehoshaphat grew exceeding rich." (v. 12)

Jehoshaphat's prosperity, like that of Asa, is not attributed to anything other than the natural consequence of following in the ways of God. (v. 4, 5) This is the same truth which Jesus taught when he said, "Seek *first* the kingdom of God, and all else shall be added unto you."

This is fundamental and should be the basis for all national security. In a world affairs reading Cayce counseled with the same principle:

> As has been indicated, if that ideal is KEPT by those who have been and are IN power, there will be kept a general trend toward greater security, greater economic considerations of the whole, greater peace, greater harmony.
>
> Not that there are not those influences that have gone about to make a beautiful condition an experience as dross, yet wherever selfishness is the prompting attitude there may be expected to be brought turmoils and strife.
>
> Where the purposes are the Prince of Peace, where "I AM my brother's keeper— I WILL do the right," these will keep and bring social security, financial security, and PEACE of mind to those that propagate same. (3976–17)

Judah had a tradition and a purpose, and kings with spiritual ideals. The kingdom of Israel, which began in rebellion, lacked that binding force.

The pattern described in this reading is clearly discernible in the leaders of both kingdoms:

> ... for without the ability to constantly hold before self the ideal as is attempted to be accomplished, man becomes as one adrift, pulled hither and yon by the various calls and cries of those who would give of this world's pleasure in fame, fortune, or what not. Let these be the outcome of a life spent in listening to the divine from within, and not the purpose of life. (239-1)

Jehoshaphat persisted in rebuilding the spiritual life of Judah. He even enlarged upon Asa's reforms and began sending teachers and priests out to instruct the people in the laws of God—perhaps even in the disciplines of meditation, that art in which the soul's forces are awakened, for in a later battle, Judah is commanded to "stand still" and watch the salvation. (2 Chronicles 20:17)

Cayce commented to the Bible class on Jehoshaphat's new practice:

> "This is the first reference we have to the sending of teachers to various parts of the land; not the first emissaries, but rather evangelists to their own people. David was the first to send missionaries. Samuel also made it a point to go from place to place to strengthen the people. He went throughout Israel from Dan to Beersheba. Now, one hundred years after David, Jehoshaphat returned to this custom."

This activity unified the people and strengthened the bonds between them, magnifying the spirit within to such an extent that "the fear of the Lord fell upon all the kingdoms of the lands that were round about

Judah, so that they made no war against Jehoshaphat."
(2 Chronicles 17:10)

Those who are familiar with the study of vibrations will sense the truth in Cayce's next remark.

> "It seems rather remarkable that the 'fear of the Lord' fell on all the heathen kingdoms around Judah, so that they refrained from fighting Jehoshaphat. We must remember, however, that since the days of Joshua the heathen had been afraid of the chosen people whenever they went to studying the law. They had a good healthy respect for God."

Power is made manifest through groups that put their trust in God. There is a corporate nature to miracles that is not overlooked in the Cayce readings. Jesus himself could do no miracles in his home town because of the unbelief. (Matthew 13:58) Priests and prophets are powerless when the spirit is blocked by doubt and fear in those to whom they minister.

As people become allied with a common goal or ideal, the more power they are able to generate and manifest—the more God's spirit can flow through them. The promise, "Where two or three are joined together in my Name, I am in the midst of same," is God's law.

Or—

> For as the people of each nation pray, AND then live that prayer, so must the Spirit work.
> (3976–23)

Ahab, Jezebel, and Jehoshaphat

Jehoshaphat followed in the ways of God, and wealth, power, and renown came as a natural consequence. As he grew "exceeding rich" he was not distracted from his spiritual ideals, but the wealth did afford temptations that led him to join forces with Ahab.

Ahab was the son of Omri, who founded Israel's fourth dynasty by slaying Zimri who had become king by murdering Elah, the son of Baasha who had come into power through his assassination of Nadab, the son of Jeroboam who "made Israel to sin."

Ahab was the son of Omri, and is introduced to the Bible story with these details: that he did evil above all those who went before him; that he wasn't content to equal the sins of Jeroboam but had to compound the evil by marrying Jezebel. (1 Kings 16:29–34)

Bible scholars disagree on Ahab, whether he was a weakling, completely dominated by Jezebel, or a strong military genius like his father who shared the same evil disposition as his wife. Cayce called him "a changeable man."

But most commentators agree upon Jezebel. She is one of the strongest female characters in ancient history, self-centered, autocratic, and determined. She has become a personification of evil. The wild license of her life became a proverb in Israel. (2 Kings 9:22) Long after she died her name remained as a by-word for all that was loathsome; in the Revelation it is given to a church in Asia Minor, suggesting a combination of fanaticism and profligacy.

Jezebel used the absolute power of her royal office to eradicate the knowledge of God and replace it with the worship of Baalism, a religion which appealed chiefly to the desires of the flesh.

Ahab inherited Omri's invincible stronghold "Samaria," a strategic fortress in the highlands of Samaria, and a strong army to go with it. The Assyrians were beginning their ascendancy into history. A cruel and ruthless people, eager for conquest, they began marching beyond the borders of Mesopotamia, intent upon world conquest. Political superpowers and ambitions of global dominion seem to be an integral part of the "latter days" cycle. The emergence of Nazi Germany, equally as savage and barbaric as the Assyrians, was the backdrop against which the world affairs readings were given.

Ahab was also threatened by his traditional enemy, the king of Damascus, perched along his northern border. Edom, Moab, and the Ammonites were additional problems. And Ahab's own kingdom was torn with unrest as Jezebel tried to forcibly implant her Phoenician religion on the Israelites, and was opposed by Elijah.

For most of his reign, Ahab was an unabashed pagan, practicing pagan rites, including child-sacrifice. During the last three years of his life, he was brought to repentance through the stern pronouncements of Elijah. (1 Kings 21) Ahab was forced to realize what his own repeated violations of moral and spiritual law had worked upon him.

Sometime during these last three years, Jehoshaphat made his overtures to Ahab. Conditions were favorable for an alliance. Jehoshaphat was rich and powerful. Ahab possessed a strategic fortress. They faced a common threat. Jehoshaphat was religious, Ahab repentant.

As the class studied the Book of Kings, Cayce commented on Jehoshaphat's move toward reconciliation.

"Although Jehoshaphat might not have been in complete sympathy with Ahab, he— being king of Judah—wanted to cooperate with the king of Israel. He knew that their strength lay in unity."

When the class reached the same episode as recorded in Chronicles, Cayce was more specific.

"This is where Jehoshaphat started on the downward path. When he was rich with worldly goods, it went to his head—he had to join up with somebody who might increase his power."

Ahab welcomed the move and invited Jehoshaphat into an alliance against the Armeneans who were threatening him.

Cayce noted that Jehoshaphat's response to Ahab reflected the same spirit as Ruth's. (Ruth 1:16)

> *"And he answered him, I will go up as you do; and my people are as your people; and my horses as your horses; and we will go to war."*
> *(2 Chronicles 18:3; 1 Kings 22:4)*

Before embarking on the campaign, Jehoshaphat asked Ahab to inquire of his prophets. All four hundred promised success.

Cayce, with his insights into human nature and spiritual processes, told this story to his class.

> "Ahab had repented to such an extent that he listened to the advice of certain prophets. Evidently the four hundred he consulted were not the very best, for Jehoshaphat apparently doubted their advice—or tried to seek further. Then Ahab told him of another prophet, Micaiah. But, because this prophet never said anything good about Ahab, Ahab wouldn't listen to him. So many of us are like Ahab in that respect. We won't listen when someone tells us something unpleasant, even though it may be the truth.
>
> "Jehoshaphat insisted on consulting Micaiah; evidently he had a premonition of the things that were to be."

A messenger was sent to summon Micaiah, and bring him to court. The messenger encouraged Micaiah to speak "pleasant" words and "prophesy good."

However, when asked by the king, Micaiah predicted that the children of Israel would lose their king and become "as sheep without a shepherd scattered on a mountain."

When Ahab blurted his irritation about this message, Micaiah revealed the full extent of his vision:

> "... I saw the Lord sitting upon his throne, and all the host of heaven standing on his right hand and on his left. And the Lord said, Who shall entice Ahab, king of Israel, that he may go up and be slain at Ramath-gilead? And one said I will entice him after this manner, and another said, I will entice him after that manner.
>
> "Then came out a spirit, and stood before the Lord, and said, I will entice him, and the Lord said, With what?
>
> "And he said, I will go out, and be a lying spirit in the mouth of all his prophets. And the Lord said, Go out and do according to what you have said." (2 Chronicles 18:18–22)

Cayce's insights continue.

> "This is the complete vision of Micaiah, indicating that all four hundred prophets had been misguided and that their information was false.
>
> "The type of spirit that Micaiah describes is common to spiritualistic seances; they're always ready to be used as messengers. Perhaps this is not an exact description of what actually happened, but Micaiah explained it in a way that the people would understand.
>
> "Zedekiah, one of the four hundred, slapped Micaiah and sarcastically asked him, 'Which way went the spirit of the Lord from me to speak to thee?' In other words, he was

making fun of Micaiah. Micaiah reminded him that he could find the answer within himself, when he sought the spirit of the Lord.

"Evidently Zedekiah had not lived what he preached. His messages from God (as he called them) were colored by Ahab's own material desires. Zedekiah was seeking favor with the king by not telling the truth as he received it. Consequently, after continuing this practice over a long period of time, he was no longer able to recognize the truth.

"Ahab became so furious with Micaiah that he put him in bonds, on bread and water, 'until I return in peace.' If he did return it would be proof the Lord had not spoken.

"We hear no more of Micaiah, but he certainly must have been released when his prophecy came true in every detail."

How shall I entice a man to his destruction? A rephrasing of Micaiah's vision might be answered with: "Surround him with those who tell him only what he wants to hear." The heart of man is basically selfish —and selfishness leads to destruction. If a man refuses to be corrected by those who know the truth, he inevitably walks toward his own collapse. No one has to plan it for him.

The subsequent scene shows that Ahab was not immune to Micaiah's presage. Inwardly he must have known it was the truth, yet believed he could escape his fate by a clever ruse.

Edgar Cayce studied the emotions of the men— and the law!

"Ahab tried to play it safe by disguising himself, so no one would know he was king. He advised Jehoshaphat to wear his royal robes, knowing the Syrians would think Jehoshaphat was king of Israel and follow him. Jehoshaphat must have felt pretty sure about Micaiah's prophecy to take the chance he did. He was a good man. He dressed in the robes and tried to lead the Syrians away from Ahab. But no man can escape his destiny—or keep from meeting himself. A chance shot hit Ahab, one not even intended for him. This reminds us of what Jesus said, 'He that attempts to save his life shall lose it.'

"Ahab's death was the end of Israel's glory. His son, Ahaziah, was such a weakling that he soon lost his foreign possessions. Moab revolted immediately."

LAST WORDS ON AHAB

Elijah's last words to Ahab foretold the complete destruction of his house. The evil acquisition of Naboth's vineyard brought forth the grim prophecy that Ahab's posterity were to be "plucked out" one by one. (1 Kings 21) Two years after Ahab's death, his son, King Ahaziah, suffered a fatal fall from the palace balcony and died in bed. Jezebel and the remaining sons were slaughtered by Jehu (the son of Nimshi), an insurgent with a divine call whom Elijah had designated. (2 Kings 9:30–37; 10:1–18)

Cayce's last words on Ahab reflect his understanding of the principles of soul-attraction and karmic involvements found in the readings, and sound a note of compassion for Ahab as well.

"After Ahab had done all the evil that could be imagined (being stirred up by Jezebel), he repented. His repentance was sincere, else God would not have stayed his punishment.

"Ahaziah, Ahab's son, became king, the

one who was to reap in his day the punishment that had been delayed for Ahab. Some might get the idea Ahab's punishment was reaped entirely by his son. Ahaziah reaped only the reward for his own sins, for Ahab—being so evil, and having such an evil wife—could only have attracted a son who was completely evil, who was meeting his own sins from some other past experience.

"On the other hand, perhaps the greatest punishment Ahab could have was to see his son suffer. That is the way most of us are—we would rather suffer ourselves than see those we love hurt.

"Ahab must have suffered greatly while anticipating all the sorrow that was to come, and mental distress is often worse than physical; but, because of his change of heart, there was peace to his people during the rest of his lifetime."

JEHOSHAPHAT REBUKED

Like Asa, his father, Jehoshaphat had to bear the rebuke of his prophets. As he returned home, victorious in battle, successfully concluding the alliance with Ahab that was to end the eighty-five years of intermittent fraternal warfare between the two kingdoms and begin an era of fifty years of peaceful co-existence, Jehu (the son of Hanan) announced to Jehoshaphat that the Lord was angry with him for joining with "the ungodly" and loving those who "hated the Lord."

The king must have instinctively known his prophet was correct. Jehoshaphat did not lash out or react from the level of his "human nature." He accepted the rebuke, and took a renewed interest in the spiritual life of his kingdom. He began instructing the judges, priests, and Levites that their activities should not be for man but for the Lord. As Jehoshaphat became immersed in his social, political, and religious reforms, his awareness and confidence grew in the Spirit. When a new threat appeared from a mighty coalition of Moabites and Ammonites, he was sufficiently cleared of his human tendency for "ungodly" alliances to face the enemy alone and through prayer.

All the men of Judah assembled in the temple court, "with their little ones, their wives, their sons, and their daughters," (2 Chronicles 20:13) while Jehoshaphat led the congregation in prayer.

Commenting on this episode, Cayce reminded his students that the succeeding miracle of deliverance was corporate in nature, the natural outcome of an integrated group consciousness.

> "Jehoshaphat offered a very beautiful prayer which, because of its sincerity and the sincerity of the people who also were seeking, brought immediate results. Always when everyone in a group seeks the Lord at the same time, something happens. If we could just remember that and try to act on it more often, our lives would be much more sane and fruitful."

Because the Spirit manifests through man's soul, Jehoshaphat's prayer aligned his and his people's consciousness with the soul-forces within. Fears and doubts were removed as the god-within was attuned to the God-without. The vibrations were raised to such a high level when Jehoshaphat concluded his prayer, asking that "God show himself," that a mighty spirit rose up in Hazaiel, a priest, who spoke with strength and power, saying, "Be not afraid, the battle is not yours, but God's." (2 Chronicles 20:15)

Hazaiel instructed Judah to go to the battlefield and "stand still," which indicates they were to take time to quiet their fears, calm the mind, and attune to the God-force and "wait for the salvation of the Lord."

When the people first demanded a monarchy, Samuel reminded them that the king would always be an expression of the spirit of the people—if they did evil, the king would be evil. If they wanted to do good, the king would follow suit. If he didn't, they had the right to change him.

The presence of a believing populace, "husbands, wives, and children" praying with the king indicates why Asa and Jehoshaphat were "good" kings. The collective faith and prayers of a seeking people must have had a strong, unseen influence on both Asa and Jehoshaphat, keeping them on the path in spite of their human failings.

The law is eternally valid. Cayce saw it in action in his day, as this reading describes:

> What, think ye, has caused or did cause that meeting of the democratic countries, or the democracies and the totalitarian states? [Treaty of Versailles, June 1919?] Was it because of the wisdom of the men that met, or that either of the four there had their own way? Rather was it not the prayers of the mothers and the fathers of each nation represented there, that there might not be that destruction of human life which would be the natural outcome of open conflict? (3976–23, June 13, 1939)

ONE BESETTING SIN

However immersed Jehoshaphat became in the social, political, and religious life of his country, he could not cure himself of his one besetting sin—alliances with "the ungodly." After Ahab's death, Jehoshaphat initiated a maritime pact with Ahaziah, Ahab's successor, and was soundly condemned by the prophet Eliezer. (2 Chronicles 20:35–37) Ahaziah's reign was brief, lasting only two years. He was succeeded by his brother Joram. When Joram came into power, he asked for Jehoshaphat's help against the king of Moab. Although Jehoshaphat had been rebuked for his alliances with Ahab and Ahaziah, he accepted Joram's request and set out on an expedition that would have cost him his life had it not been for Elisha. (2 Kings 3)

After a seven-day march in the wilderness, the expedition was ready to perish for lack of water. Joram, troubled by his conscience, felt the situation was requiting all for their sins. The godly Jehoshaphat calmly asked that a prophet be found who could give guidance. Elisha was nearby and volunteered. Elisha said he would not give aid to the king of Israel, but Jehoshaphat was worth saving. Elisha called for a minstrel, and while he played, the prophet entered into deep meditation and envisioned an unusual strategy which proved successful.

Although there was a materialistic aspect to Jehoshaphat's alliances, Cayce saw spiritual overtones as well. In speaking of Jehoshaphat's last battle, he commented:

> "When Joram came into power, the first thing he did was take a census, to see how many fighting men he had. Then he besought Jehoshaphat to join forces with him as he had done for Ahab. Jehoshaphat's answer again reminds us of Ruth. That's why he was called the great Jehoshaphat. He tried to unite the divided kingdoms, so they would again be as one. However, the kings of Israel did not have the same ideal. They wanted unity for material reasons alone. They did not consider the spiritual advantages or God's original purpose."

Cayce summarized the life of this great man with a few brief comments and lessons.

"Jehoshaphat was a good man; he made peace with Ahab, and later with Ahaziah, and did everything that was right; except he, too, failed to take away the offerings in the high places. No doubt this had become an impossibility as far as any one king is concerned. Every now and then we have this statement to remind us that no matter how good the king was, '. . . nevertheless the high places were not taken away.' One especially good thing Jehoshaphat did was to get rid of the remnant of the Sodomites, which his father Asa had failed to do.

"It seems that Jehoshaphat's only besetting sin was evil associations. He did all right as long as he sought God and stayed away from evil companions. But, immediately when he became associated with those who did wickedly, he was drawn from the correct path. Many of us are like that today. It's easy to be good when it is all smooth sailing; when everyone agrees and swims along with us. But when we come up against an obstacle such as people of prominence who disagree with us, we feel weak and unstable. We don't stick to what we believe, regardless."

3

Elijah and Elisha

AHAB, JEZEBEL, AND ELIJAH

Introductory details are given in the Bible about Ahab and Jezebel. Ahab did evil above all those before him, built altars to Baal, served idols, added to his abominations by child-sacrifice, and provoked the Lord to more anger than any of his predecessors. (1 Kings 16:30–34)

Jezebel came from a prominent family. She was a Phoenician princess, the daughter of Ethbaal, king of the Zidonians.

But Elijah appears in the story without warning or introduction. The Bible only notes where he came from —Tishbeh, the location of which is uncertain.

Elijah is the archetype of the Hebrew prophet, strong, courageous, unable to compromise with sin, terrible in his denunciations.

He appears in Israel when the nation has passed the point where self-preservation is possible. Abijah, the prophet who anointed Jeroboam, had the first grim insight into Israel's national destiny. He predicted that the new kingdom would be "uprooted and scattered" and be no more. (1 Kings 4)

The spiritual deterioration which had taken place under Solomon, coupled with Jeroboam's example, proved too powerful an influence for the ten tribes to overcome. None of Israel's kings had the moral, mental, or spiritual development to offset the national trend that was set, apparently, in Jeroboam's lifetime.

The kingdom was doomed because of the path it chose to follow, and Ahab and Jezebel were a natural part of the fabric. Although Jezebel forced Baalism on the people, it had been a popular religion even before her lifetime. The sensuous rites of a fertility cult were forever distracting the Israelites. But the Spirit had not given up. Elijah was called to be the counterthrust to Jezebel, putting before a backsliding and wayward people the knowledge and power of the One God.

EDGAR CAYCE ON ELIJAH

Edgar Cayce's acceptance of reincarnation enabled him to be an able interpreter of the law of karma, or cause and effect. His psychic sensitivities brought deep spiritual insights into all phases of life, and he took this understanding to his study of the Bible. His approach in the Bible class was almost deceptively casual and very low-keyed. His pragmatic and "homespun" delivery shows the influence of the rural Kentucky farmland where he was born and raised, but the spiritual laws which undergird each lesson are universal and eternal, reflecting his own highly perceptive and developed sensitivity.

When he discussed Elijah and his bitter conflict with Jezebel, he did not highlight the dramatic elements of the story, or stress the struggle between good and evil, as so many commentators have been led to discuss and expound upon so profoundly and so well. His lectures reflect rather his concern that the Bible study be rooted in the experiences of everyday life. Thus he chose as his lesson the weaknesses of Elijah and his fears, and how the Lord was trying to make him strong, something the students knew was happening in their lives too.

Elijah shows great strength and unswerving conviction when dealing with Ahab or fighting against Baalism. He first appears in the Bible directed by God's word to forecast to Ahab the coming of a drought in Israel. The Lord then instructs Elijah where to go for the duration of the drought, where he remains in hiding for three years, coming out only when it is time to announce the end of the plague.

Elijah summoned Ahab to gather together all the people of Israel and all the prophets of Baal to the top of Mt. Carmel for a test. He challenged the prophets of Baal to prove their god was superior to Jehovah, but not before he rebuked the Israelites for "limping with two different opinions."

He denounced the people for forsaking God and chastised them with his boast,

"I, even I only, remain a prophet of the Lord."
(1 Kings 18:22)

Elijah challenged the priests of Baal to prepare a ritual sacrifice, a burnt offering, but with no fire. Elijah would do the same, and each would call upon their god to answer with fire. The god who answered would be the true God.

The priests of Baal prepared the altar and prayed and called to Baal all day, with no response. By evening they had begun to cut and slash themselves with knives, hoping to get Baal's attention with their pain and mortification. All their efforts were futile and Elijah truly enjoyed their frustration.

When Elijah prepared his altar in the evening, he had the altar, the offering, and the wood soaked three times with water. He ordered a trench dug around the altar and filled with water. Then he called to Jehovah, who answered him with a great fire that consumed the altar, the offering, the wood, and even "licked up" the water in the trench.

The people were convinced with this demonstration. Elijah ordered the prophets of Baal seized. Not one of the four hundred escaped. They were taken to the brook Kishon and killed.

Apparently this was all done in the presence of a powerless Ahab. The test on Mt. Carmel coincided with the end of the drought. Elijah said to Ahab, *"Go . . . for there is the rushing sound of rain . . . Mount your horse, and get down before the rain stops you."* (1 Kings 18:41, 44)

Up to this point we have an inspiring and unparalleled story of one man's faith, courage, and unswerving loyalty and trust in his God. No hint of fear or weakness is present.

Ahab rode swiftly to Jezreel and arrived ahead of the winds and the black clouds which brought a driving rain, and reported immediately to Jezebel. When she heard of the happenings on Mt. Carmel and the loss of her priests, she dispatched a messenger to Elijah with a proclamation that she would have his life "about this time tomorrow."

Elijah's reaction has fascinated students of the Bible ever since.

"And Elijah was afraid, and he arose and fled for his life." (1 Kings 19:3)

A WOMAN'S WRATH

He fled for one day with his disciples, and then, apparently to be able to travel faster, he left them behind and continued for another day alone. What was he running from? It wasn't death he feared, for that night he prayed, "Lord, take away my life." He was afraid of Jezebel!

"Elijah was a prophet who could stand up to four hundred priests," Cayce told the class, "but he couldn't face the wrath of a woman." He escaped Jezebel's revenge, but he eventually had to face that woman again,

Cayce suggested, and met that fear within himself in a later incarnation as John the Baptist!

It is not surprising that Cayce saw in the relationship between Elijah and Jezebel a karmic pattern which he assumed was something brought over from previous incarnations. His assumption that Elijah later incarnated as John the Baptist was based upon a Biblical prophecy, support from a reading, and the testimony of Jesus. This enabled Cayce to see the karmic entanglement continued in a New Testament setting.

He told his class:

> "In the last chapter of Malachi we are told, 'Behold, I will send you Elijah the prophet before the coming of the great and dreadful day of the Lord.' (Malachi 4:5) In the 11th of Matthew we have Christ's testimony concerning John, 'For this is he of whom it is written, Behold I will send my messenger to prepare the way before thee! . . . and if ye will receive it, he [John] is Elijah, who was to come.' "

The connection between Elijah and John is stated in reading 262–87 and repeated in 3054–4, and drawn most clearly in 1158–6:

> Did not John come as the voice of one crying in the wilderness and in the spirit of Elijah? Yet he *was* Elijah. (1158–6)

The readings instruct us that what are normally considered hardships, and difficult problems in life, in reality give us chances to overcome our limitations and present opportunities for soul growth. If Elijah was subject to fear of women, or a woman, Jezebel offered him the greatest "opportunity" for overcoming it. His devotion to God should have supplied the strength to surmount his weakness. But in John we find the same fault:

> For even in Elijah or John we find the faltering, the doubting. We find no faltering, no doubting, no putting aside of the purpose in the Master Jesus. (3054-4)

Harmony with God's spirit, which is the universal spirit of love, patience, and mercy, leads to grace, and in grace all karma is erased. Self-will, rather than God's will, is the source of all our hardships.

The absence of God's command, ordering Elijah to slay Jezebel's prophets, impressed Cayce. This intimated to the seer that Elijah may have been acting on his own initiative, rather than performing God's will, thus building a negative karmic pattern.

Cayce asked his class:

> "Was Elijah commanded to kill the prophets of Baal? It is not indicated that he was, but he did. Evidently a personal animosity was involved, which Elijah had to meet at a future date—perhaps as John the Baptist."

Elijah's mockery and great delight over the frustration and failure of the prophets of Baal are other indications suggesting deep-seated personal and emotional drives which may have colored and misguided his directions from high spiritual life.

Cayce assumed Herodias, the wife of Herod, was a later incarnation of Jezebel. When she ordered the beheading of John, she obtained her revenge and the karmic wheel completed a full cycle.

Cayce philosophized to the class:

> "Jezebel's threat was to take Elijah's life on the morrow. She intended just that, but

sometimes it takes us several hundred years to realize our tomorrows.

"Eventually Jezebel had Elijah's head cut off, as she promised she would."

ANOTHER KARMIC LESSON
(1 Kings 2)

The final episode in Elijah's struggle with members of Ahab's family drew additional commentary by Cayce on the possible basis of a karma sown by Elijah which was reaped by John.

When Ahaziah, Ahab's son and successor, fell from his balcony and was severely injured, he sent messengers to the priests of Baal for a remedy. The messengers were turned back by Elijah who told them to instruct the king that he would never rise from his bed, but would die in it. The messengers returned and reported to Ahaziah. Ahaziah recognized Elijah from their description and sent them out with orders to bring the prophet to him.

When the messengers arrived with the summons, Elijah's response was unprecedented. He did one thing at which he excelled—called down fire! and the messengers were consumed.

Cayce saw the effects of this coming back on John.

"It is hard to understand Elijah's actions with the messengers of Ahaziah. It appears as if he was afraid of going to Ahaziah and was using his power wrongly when he called down fire to consume those men. We can't conceive of this being God's way. Of course we have no way of knowing Ahaziah's purpose in sending for Elijah. He may have wanted to put Elijah to death. Or Ahaziah may have intended to beseech the Lord, through Elijah, to give him another chance.

Anyway, we can be sure Elijah had to meet his acts. The time came when, as John the Baptist, he was put to death and no one, including Jesus, saved him from it. Jesus could have, but John was meeting himself. From our previous studies, we have learned that the meeting of self sometimes requires death itself.

"In other words, it was necessary for John to die this way in order for him to have the awakening he needed. Remember, Jesus said that the least in the kingdom was greater than John, because John was not aware of his own purpose even though he had prophesied about the purpose of others.

"John was expecting Jesus, whom he had proclaimed as the Saviour, to save him from physical death. But it was through his death that John met and overcame his own shortcomings. That, for John, was his cross—at that particular period; just as we each today have our individual crosses to bear. No one can save us from them, but if we try to understand WHY we have them, and seek the aid of the Christ, they become easier to bear."

The basis for this interpretation is found in 3976-27, a world affairs reading.

... even as He gave to that one who had announced by the authority of the prophets, "Behold the Lamb of God that taketh away the sins of the world," who comes to bring peace into the hearts of those who seek to do righteousness in the earth. And yet because he had fallen into that answering as of self to fears within, he began to doubt—as apparently no measure was being attempted, outwardly at least, to relieve him of his bonds; and he asked, "Art thou He that was to come, or shall we look for another?" The Master's answer is the judgment of today, even as then. There was not the Yes or No answer, but "Go tell John that the sick are healed, the poor have the gospel preached, the lame walk, the blind see." (3976–27)

The episode with Ahaziah's messengers is the last recorded act in Elijah's life, but not his final appearance in Scripture. Malachi prophesied his return as John the Baptist. But even after John's beheading, Elijah reappeared with Moses on the mount of transfiguration (Matthew 7:3) to discuss with Jesus how holy powers "might be entrusted into the keeping of men and women everywhere." (1809–1) The presence of Elijah on the mount of transfiguration was a message in itself to the onlookers, indicating "that they, too, would become as messengers to a waiting world." (262–87)*

THE STILL SMALL VOICE

And behold, the Lord passed by, and a great and strong wind rent the mountains and broke in pieces the rocks before the Lord; but the Lord was not in the wind; and after the wind an earthquake; but the Lord was not in the earthquake:

And after the earthquake a fire; but the Lord was not in the fire; and after the fire a still small voice.

And when Elijah heard it, he wrapped his

---

*Moses' part on the mount of transfiguration was to talk with Jesus about "what manner of means there would be for the bringing of the awareness and consciousness into the hearts and minds and lives of the children of men" and "what the death, the passing on the cross might mean." (1809–1) Moses' presence meant to those apostles who were present "a definite undertaking which set them apart from other peoples." (262–87)

face in his mantle and went and stood at the en-
trance of the cave. (1 Kings 19:11, 12)

Elijah's hegira from Jezebel lasted forty days and forty nights and took him to Mt. Sinai, the holy mount where Moses talked to God. Here, in the recesses of a cave, Elijah confessed his fears to God: "They seek my life, to take it away."

Meditation, dreams, and prayer are the means by which man attunes his consciousness to God and gets to be on speaking terms with his own soul. While meditating in his cave, Elijah had the deeply moving vision about the forces of nature and the still small voice, a spiritual experience which must have changed the course of his life.

Spiritual experiences, as universal and elemental as Elijah's, move on many different levels, and, to the person who receives them, bring new insight and vision into all aspects of life. In other words, Elijah was not only being confirmed in the truth about God, but was also being told something about himself. Dreams and visions from the divine come, as the readings tell us, not only for inspiration and revelation, but for correction and guidance.

No doubt Elijah was seeing himself in this experience. His demonstration on Mt. Carmel and his action against Ahaziah's messengers are revealing, and indicate Elijah set great store in his own psychic abilities. He had the power to perform "great wonders" and to call down fire.

In the Revelation, the disciple of love, John, writes that it is within the power of the beast (or carnal man) "to perform great wonders" to such an extent as to even "make fire come down from heaven on earth," which beguiles men and causes them "to make an image to the beast." (Revelation 13:13)

The "beast" is the symbol for the lower nature of man, the unruly emotions, and might even include psychic power that is not spiritually directed. Cayce suggested, as we have seen, that Elijah may not have been entirely spirit-led in his actions against the priests of Baal, but acting through personal animosities. Those who can perform "great wonders" inevitably set the examples which influence others in forming their concepts of God. If the example set indicates that God is the phenomenon rather than spirit, or consents to the wholesale murder of unbelievers, this makes for an "image to the wild beast," rather than the still, small voice.

Elijah must have gone deep into the soul to have the experience he did. Perhaps his revelation brought to his mind that he was closer to the true spirit of Jehovah when he gently filled the widow's cruse and quietly restored her son (1 Kings 17:9-24) than when he challenged the priests of Baal or called down fire on Ahaziah's messengers.

We find this interpretation in the readings:

> Think not, even as He, to do some great deed that would make the welkin ring throughout the earth. Rather KNOW it is the little line, the little precept, the little lesson given into the lives and experiences that brings the awareness into the hearts and souls of men and women; that consciousness of the NEARNESS in the still small voice within.
>
> For as proclaimed of old, it is not in the thunder or lightning, it is not in the storm, it is not in the loudness—but the still small voice within!
>
> So as ye write, so as ye talk, so as ye love—let it be in meekness of spirit, in PURPOSEFULNESS of service, in an activity and an eye single to the GLORY of the Father through those that are His children. (1472-3)

The same principle is restated in this reading:

> For know, it is not the great deeds one performs that make for the building of hope

in the hearts and minds of those you meet, nor the mere satisfaction of a self-aggrandizing experience; but it is that which *creates* hope—that which makes for the expression of patience, long-suffering, grace, mercy and truth! THESE are the things that build into the hearts of men, EVERYWHERE, harmony and peace and hope! (1574–1)

Elijah learned a great lesson. The truth he encountered must have upset and challenged some of his set opinions. God is the spirit of truth, while men are hedged in, prejudiced, and blinded by their emotions. Only those who seek, through meditation, to attune the conscious mind to the God-within through periods of silence, like Elijah, can overcome the limitations of the self and gain the greater understanding of their souls.

Cayce's presentation to the Bible class rested with this lesson.

"The elements obeyed Jesus. They were used by Him; yet these are the things of which man is most fearful. However, we are reminded again and again that it is the still, small voice that can do the most, not only in our physical selves but in the effect we may have, or may make, upon the lives of others, according to the purpose of those who stop and listen.

"Our relationship to God is bound to be individual. It becomes a personal thing for us to know God, and we can only know Him by answering the still, small voice within."

THE SCHOOL OF PROPHETS

Those who studied the Cayce readings were well acquainted with the religious sect in Judaism called the "Essenes" long before the discovery of the Dead Sea

Scrolls. Several decades before the discovery at Qumram, the life readings described in great detail the practice, beliefs, purposes, and many of the personalities who were involved in this prophetic and mystical cult to which Joseph, Jesus, and Mary belonged.

Describing the Essenes at the time of Jesus, one reading states, ". . . their purpose was of the first foundations of the prophets as established, or as understood from the school of prophets, by Elijah." (254–109)

The site of the school of prophets, as well as the later Essene center, was on Mt. Carmel.

> . . . in Carmel—the original place where the school of prophets was established during Elijah's time. (5749–8)

This reading indicates by inference that the occult was studied by the prophets.

> . . . these were called then Essenes; and those that were students of what ye would call astrology, numerology, phrenology, and those phases of that study of the return of individuals—or [re-]incarnation . . . [and] that certain periods were a cycle . . . (5749–8)

Both the Essenes and the School of Prophets grew from the same roots.

> . . . the group we refer to here as the Essenes, which was the outgrowth of the periods of preparations from the teachings by Melchizedek, as propagated by Elijah, and Elisha and Samuel. These were set aside for preserving themselves in a direct line of choice for the offering of themselves as channels through which there might come the new or the divine origin, see? (254–109)

This reading, although describing an incarnation at the time of Jesus, states specifically what Elijah taught, and infers what his approach may have been.

> The entity was closely associated with the priests who were active in the Carmelian area, where there had been the early teachings established years ago by Elijah, Elisha, Samuel; *that taught the mysteries of man and his relationships to those forces as might manifest from within and without.*
>
> The entity then was among the sages who chose the young that were to be set apart as channels through which that blessing might come to the world [the Divine Birth] ...
>
> *These brought at times periods when the entity needed long periods of meditation, and the setting aside of activities necessary to induce the submerging of the physical to the spiritual in its relationships to materialization.* (2520–1) [Italics added]

This extract, also from the New Testament period. offers additional insight into the original practice of the school of prophets:

> ... the Essenes ... cherished not merely the conditions that had come as word of mouth but had kept the records of the periods when individuals had been visited with the supernatural or out of the ordinary experiences; whether in dreams, visions, voices, or what not that had been and were felt by these students of the customs, of the law, of the activities throughout the experiences of this peculiar people—the promises and the many ways these had been interpreted by those to whom the preservation of same had been committed. (1472–3)

It is not certain when Elijah established the school of prophets. Until his experience with the still, small voice on Carmel, he believed, and had boldly asserted before God and his fellow man, that he was the last remaining, and only, true prophet in Israel. (1 Kings 18:22; 19:10, 14) Certainly the school couldn't have been established before this.

The readings describe the earmarks of a genuine spiritual experience:

> Seek experiences not as experiences alone but as purposefulness. For what be the profit to thyself, to thy neighbor, if experiences alone of such natures rack thy body— owing to its high vibration—without being able to make thee . . . a better neighbor, a better individual in every manner? *These* be the fruits, that it makes thee kinder, gentler, stronger in body, in mind, in purpose to *be* a channel through which the love of *God* . . . may be manifested in the world. Not as a vision, an experience alone. (281–27)

A spiritual experience is necessarily humbling to the carnal ego, but strengthening to the soul. Although Elijah testified that he was the last and only prophet in Israel, he learned through the still, small voice that there were seven thousand others in Israel who "had not bowed to Baal." (1 Kings 19) Elijah was not alone.

The experience on the mountain altered and broadened Elijah's vision, renewed his courage, calmed his fears, and added a new dimension to his ministry. It would not be the only time a vision has changed the course of a great man's life.

Perhaps by becoming aware of the other seven thousand "good men" in Israel he was inspired to seek out the faithful and begin the school of prophets.

Although Elijah saw the wind, the earthquake, and

the fire, it wasn't until he reached the still center of the soul that he received guidance.

He was told to go down from the mountain and back into the world and anoint Hazael as king over the Syrians, to raise up Jehu to replace Ahab, and to seek out Elisha and accept him as his student and successor to his prophetic office.

Although there were always prophets in Israel—Abraham himself is given the title—from this time on they begin to rise like a fresh current of living water in a polluted stream: Elisha, Isaiah, Joel, Jeremiah, Hoshea, Amos, and others less known, and some completely anonymous.

Although the presence of so many gifted seers can be explained as a purely spontaneous happening born out of the stress and trauma of a national decline, it is interesting to consider that this waxing prophetic impulse was channeled and directed through a school headed by Elijah.

A Georgia woman was told that in a previous incarnation she had been "the daughter of that prophet" and was exposed to all the activities of the period.

> Before that the entity was in the Holy Land among those of the household of the prophet during the period of Ahab's and Jezebel's rule in the land.
>
> The entity then was the daughter of that prophet,* in the name Adah. The entity knew trials, the entity knew the wrath of those surrounding the entity and those periods of turmoils and wickedness among those in high places. Yet the entity kept the faith through the period.
>
> The entity was acquainted with the activities of Jehu and the entity's sister.

---

*Edgar Cayce, in his correspondence, expressed the opinion that the "prophet" referred to in this reading was Obadiah (see I Kings 18:3).

The entity kept the faith and saw the fulfilling of the prophet's words about Ahab, Jezebel, and those people of that day.

Hence the prophecies as well as the promises throughout the Book have meant and do mean much to the entity. (4065-1)

EDGAR CAYCE ON ELISHA

And it came to pass when the Lord was about to take Elijah up to heaven by a whirlwind, ... Elijah said to Elisha, Ask what I shall do for you before I am taken away from you. And Elisha said, Let a double portion of your spirit be upon me. (2 Kings 2:9)

Elisha was able to receive the boon because he fulfilled the conditions which Elijah put about it.

And he said, You have asked too much; nevertheless, if you see me when I am taken from you, it shall be so to you; but if not, it shall not be so. (2 Kings 2:10)

Then came the test.

And it came to pass, as they still went on and talked, behold, there appeared a chariot of fire and horses of fire, and separated the two; and Elijah went up by a whirlwind into heaven.
And Elisha saw it and he cried, My father, my father, the chariot of Israel and the horsemen thereof. And he saw him no more. (2 Kings 2:11, 12)

Was this the death of Elijah? his translation? (as with Enoch, Genesis 5:24) or a transfiguration, like Jesus' on the mount? (Matthew 7:2, Mark 9:2)

Whichever it was, it marked an end to the dramatic ministry of Elijah and the beginning of Elisha's.

Cayce drew a few lessons from the prelude to the ascension (2 Kings 2:1–8), and offered his reasons why as a demonstration of the spiritual forces in man, it could be considered the "high point" in the Old Testament.

He told his class:

"We have a lesson in perseverence in Elisha. He would not give up. Evidently the school of prophets had predicted that Elijah would ascend, and fifty sons of prophets—that is, students, the same as Elisha—followed Elijah at a distance, hoping to see the ascension when it took place. Elisha didn't mingle with them, but stuck close to Elijah, refusing to be left behind. It was necessary that he be consistent and persistent.

"Here, possibly, is the high point in the Old Testament. Together these two individuals were capable of generating the most powerful force that had ever yet been manifested in the flesh."

The chariot arose, and Elijah threw down his mantle. When Elisha picked up the mantle and put it on his shoulders, he received the "double portion." Thus began the ministry of the man whose miracles are second only to Jesus'.

Elisha

In a remarkable reading for a four-year-old child some astounding information was given. Three outstanding incarnations were described. If the reading is correct, the entity who had been Noah, or ". . . that one to whom was entrusted man's advent into the world," was also the same who later incarnated as Elisha.

The influences of that prophetic life were described for the parents:

> ... the entity was that one upon whom the mantle of Elijah fell—who in his material activity performed more unusual acts, or miracles, that are only comparable with the Master himself.
>
> The entity then as Elisha brought into the experience much that was of the unusual in expression.
>
> So in the present, in the experiences of this entity, there may be expected just as unusual expression; as those coming to the entity to receive the blessings from the handkerchief, the photograph even, or those things that the entity may touch or bless ...
>
> Here we may see a demonstration, an illustration of that which has been indicated or intimated through these channels, as of a PERFECT channel being formed for the advent of an entity-soul that would bring blessings to all—IF there is the directing of the developing years ...
>
> Do not allow the entity, in the first ten to twelve years, to get away from the spiritual truths in the Old and the New Testaments; not as an ism, not as a cult. For it will be easy for a cult, an ism, to be formed about the entity and its prognostications. But rather let it be as one glorifying the truths that are promised in the thirtieth of Deuteronomy, and in the fourteenth, fifteenth, sixteenth, and seventeenth chapters of John. These impress. Accredit the entity's abilities to these sources. When there are questions as to the source from which the entity obtains its information, agree that it comes from the infinite. For these are the developments. (2547–1)

Cayce's lessons to the Bible class reveal a great admiration for the prophet.

> "No other character in all the Bible, other than Jesus, performed so many miracles as Elisha, or was in the midst of so many unusual happenings. Practically every type of miracle we can imagine was performed by Elisha. We don't credit this to any special thing in Elisha save as a 'double portion' of Elijah's spirit, or because Elijah's mantle fell on his shoulders.
>
> "Except where he cursed the children and they were eaten up by the bears, he was one of the most consistent of all prophets in the Old Testament. He never, never refused help to anyone, and never asked for or accepted anything for himself. If it hadn't been for that one thing with the children, it seems as if he would have been perfect."

The incident with the children occurred shortly after Elisha received his "double portion" of spirit, and is recorded in 2 Kings 2.

> *. . . and as he was going up along the way, there came forth little boys out of the city and mocked him, saying Go up, you bald head, go up, you bald head.*
> *And he turned back and saw them and cursed them in the name of the Lord. And there came forth two she-bears out of the forest, and tore forty-two of the boys. (2 Kings 2:23–24)*

Just as the readings enabled Cayce to see the karmic pattern from Elijah to John, the readings also enabled him to look back upon a cause and effect relationship between Elisha and Noah.

He told the Bible class:

"Remember, Elisha was a reincarnation of Noah, as indicated in the readings. He made good all the way. The only activity that seems uncalled for was the cursing of the little children who made fun of his bald head. How quickly human nature reacts! These incidents give us a glimpse of the human nature of these individuals and shows how much God has to overlook. If we realize this, it should be easier to overlook faults in others and not condemn them, thus glorifying God the more.

"We recall that Noah cursed his own grandson, apparently for just such a minor offense. The human nature in the individual hadn't changed one iota from the time of Noah. We can easily imagine that these children might have been reminders of that other day when he had warned the people about going into the ark and they made fun of him. Sometimes, no matter how good we try to be, we lose ourselves for the moment and in anger undo what it has taken us centuries to build. That is the human trait we must overcome.

"It is a consolation that such holy men, in direct contact with God, fell down occasionally. No wonder we fall by the wayside. That's the price we pay by being in the flesh."

MISUSE OF POWER

The readings always counseled individuals seeking power—whether it was psychic, spiritual, economic, social, political, or whatever—to know their ideals and be sure of their purpose.

When Elijah left in the whirlwind, he didn't "leave" his spirit, but gave Elisha a technique, or tool, to open up his own spiritual centers. When Jesus ascended, he didn't take his spirit with him, but said, "My spirit I leave with you." The spirit is everywhere. It does not come and go. Elijah's mantle was the material means which enabled Elisha, through his faith, to attune to his soul's forces. Jesus gave us His promise that through faith in His word we would be able to raise our consciousness to the divine within and do "greater works." (John 14:12)

Perhaps when Elisha received his "double portion" he was not well-grounded in his responsibility for its constructive uses. Being so newly (and suddenly) invested with such a large amount of psychic energy, when the children laughed, he reacted with his human nature and abused his gift.

A reference to Elisha, and a philosophy about power, is developed in this reading for a lawyer, who was seeking to develop his psychic abilities to gain an advantage in the stock market:

> Look at those . . . money powers of the earth. And look at what their bodies, minds, and souls are today! Are ye willing, then, to pay such a price?
> Are ye willing that such shall be thine OWN temptation? that ye are to build within thine experience that which will give thee, in thine own personal self, the right to say Yea and Nay to thy brother in want here and there?
> Are ye willing to take, rather, that of knowledge—as Elisha, thine OWN helpmeet oft—and . . . use same in such a manner as that the lowliest, yea those in authority, yea thy fellow man that ye meet day by day will call thee blessed?
> Or is it POWER alone ye seek?
> As to the manners then—these ye MUST determine within thine OWN consciousness;

and these ye would weigh well with thy purposes through this material experience.

For know, ye ARE constantly meeting thine OWN self! Not that an individual is not to be endowed with purposes, desires, and the like in relationship to his fellow man—or to conditions of every nature whether they be social, economic, political, or what not. But for what purpose are these positions chosen by thyself?

Are ye to keep well-balanced? Are ye to keep the influences and the activities in those directions in which ye may know ever that thy purpose is that the glory of the Father-God is to be daily manifested in thy dealings with thy fellow man?

Or are ye to become a lord, a god within thine own right; that ye may say to this one, "Go," or to this one, "Stay," and he doeth it? (826–9)

4

Bad News for Judah

Jehoshaphat cemented the alliance between Judah and Israel through the marriage of his son, Jehoram, to Athaliah, Ahab's daughter. Although Jehoshaphat did much that was "right" in the sight of God, he was soundly rebuked by the prophets for his besetting weakness for "ungodly" alliances. His alliance with Israel may have been brilliant politically, but it eventually resulted in Jezebel's daughter sitting on David's throne, with nearly fatal consequences for the Davidic line.

Jehoram was as dominated by his wife as Ahab had been by her mother. When Jehoram became king, he became an advocate of Baalism and a persecutor of those who opposed him. His first act was to order the murder of his six brothers.

The sixty years of peace and security which Judah enjoyed, through the moral and spiritual leadership of Asa and Jehoshaphat, soon dissolved as Jehoram began forsaking and forgetting God. Edom revolted and the Philistines and Arabians invaded the country. Jehoram lost all his sons in the fighting, except one. After an eight-year reign, Jehoram died of a horrible disease—"his bowels fell out." (2 Chronicles 21:19)

Ahaziah, the surviving son, succeeded his father

and ruled for one year until he was slain by Jehu, who had been designated by Elijah, and anointed by Elisha, to purge the evils of the house of Ahab from the land.

Jehu extinguished the house of Ahab from Israel and began a new dynasty. And Athaliah was intent upon establishing her dynasty in Jerusalem.

With Ahaziah's death, Athaliah became the queen of Judah, and her first act was to order the murder of all her sons and grandsons.

The prophets were vindicated who had rebuked Jehoshaphat. The dangerous consequences of his alliances had come full cycle.

But, because God is a universal consciousness, and a part of His mind is in every soul, Athaliah's plans were thwarted. Jehoshabeath, the daughter of Jehoram, was inspired to move swiftly and courageously. She concealed one of Amaziah's young sons, Joash, and kept him hidden for six years in her bed chambers while Athaliah reigned. After six years, Joash was taken out of hiding and crowned in the temple by Jehoiadah, the high priest and husband of Jehoshabeath. Athaliah was overthrown and the Davidic dynasty reinstated.

SATAN BOUND, SATAN LOOSENED

In Revelation 20, Satan is cast into a great pit and chained for a thousand years, and then loosened "for a season." This prophecy, the readings tell us, is symbolic of cycles which come in man's experience. The anti-Christ spoken of by John in the Revelation is nothing other than the spirit of hate, which breeds strife, selfishness, egoism, contention, and other fruits which can take possession of individuals, groups, and masses.

The devil, or "Satan," is the spirit in man which is in rebellion against God's laws of love, joy, obedience, kindness, and long-suffering. This devil has no strength except through man's weakness. (281-16)

Many times was "Satan bound" in the Old Testament. When the Israelites were strong in their search for God and had a will to live according to God's laws, the devil was powerless. Under Joshua, the people suppressed their rebellious spirit and worked long and hard for constructive ends. Under the moral and spiritual leadership of Ahaz and Jehoshaphat, the "devil" was kept in chains for sixty years, only to be let loose through Jehoram's bad conduct.

In his weakness Abraham was almost deceived into destroying his only son. If he had, the plan of salvation would have been thwarted. Absalom's rebellion almost destroyed David's kingdom before it was established and its principal work—the temple—begun. If it had, the whole pattern of spiritual revelation would have been upset and delayed. Because of Jehoshaphat's "one besetting sin" Athaliah sat on David's throne and used the opportunity to destroy his heirs.

The jealousy of Joseph's brothers, Saul's gloomy moods, Absalom's pride, and Jehoshaphat's alliances were all avenues through which the destructive forces could move: and would have been successful had they not been overturned by faith.

The readings indicate that the "devil" is always kept in chains as long as men seek to do God's will first and foremost.

> Thus is Satan bound, thus is Satan banished from the earth. The desire to do evil is only of him. And when there are . . . those only whose desire and purpose of their heart is to glorify the Father, these will be those periods when this shall come to pass.

> Be YE *ALL* DETERMINED within thy minds, thy hearts, thy purposes, to be of that number! (281–37).

JEHU: THE CORRUPTION OF A CALL

> *Then Elisha the prophet called one of the sons of the prophets and said to him, Gird up your*

*loins and take this flask of oil in your hand and go
to Ramath-gilead;*

*And when you get there, look for Jehu the
son of Jimshi, and go in and make him arise up
from among his brethren, and bring him into an
inner chamber;*

*Then take the flask of oil and pour it on his
head, and say to him, Thus says the Lord, I have
anointed you king over my people Israel.*

*Then open the door and flee, and do not tarry.
(2 Kings 9:1–3)*

In the world affairs readings, we find another
startling lesson in Edgar Cayce's story of the Old
Testament. Hitler was said to be in the same position,
relatively, toward the Jews as Jehu, another Old Testament dictator with a "divine call."

Q–6. Is Hitler psychically led?
A–6. Psychically led; for the understanding of
psychic is that the relationships between the
mental activities and the source and the spiritual influences are being directed, or *are* directing, the physical activities of the body.
Hence it may be said that he is psychically
led, for he is called for a purpose as has been
given; not only in the affairs of a nation, but
as in the affairs of the world. And he stands
much in the position as did Jehu, as regards
that people that *think* themselves oppressed.
(3976–13) (November 4, 1933)

The name Hitler is now a "proverb and by-word"
for inhuman cruelty, megalomania, barbarism, and fanaticism. It is hard for the modern mind to think of
Hitler as anything but the ultimate incarnation of evil,
yet reading 3976–13 implies that even then, 1933, Hitler
had the opportunity to fulfill a divine call. The reading

states this overtly and through the association with Jehu, who had been "raised up" by Elisha (1 Kings 19:16) and anointed by Elisha (2 Kings 9), two of the greatest psychics of the Old Testament.

Like all souls, Hitler had the ability to choose between good and evil. The reading tells us he could have brought "light to the world," and states he was "psychically led" and "called for a purpose." The reading also declares that his policies were "initiated . . . from spiritual sources" and "gained through deep meditation."

Clearly, in these respects, he shares much in common with many of the Old Testament leaders.

From the cosmic level of consciousness from which Cayce drew his information while giving a reading, the seer described Hitler as an entity of force, power and destiny.

> It would be well that each interested in the policies, and in which is the directing influence in the life of the dictator or of Hitler, study that which has been the impelling infleunce in the *man*—as a man, in the mind as it acceded to power; *for few does power not destroy, as men. Yet this man, unless there is material change, will survive even that. (3976–14)* [Italics added]

Indeed, the Old Testament prophets, such as Elijah and Elisha, must have sensed and seen the presence of a similar power and destiny in the men they selected and supported for carrying out God's purposes in the earth. Yet they prophesied and supported only with the conditional "if." We have no record as to the prophecies and conditions laid out for Jehu, but we do have Cayce's warning on Hitler.

> If the power is held in that line as it has been directed in the present . . . there will

rise a new ideal in the hearts, in the minds of the people.

If imperialism among the people is kept in abeyance, great may be the rewards to this peoples, this nation . . . (3976–13)

Although this reading was emphatic about Hitler's opportunity to fulfill a divine mission, the association in 1933 with Jehu was, for a student of the Bible, grimly prophetic.

A REIGN OF TERROR

"Unimaginable horror and loathing . . . merciless butchery, reeking with blood . . . a dreadful nightmare, a lurid picture of brutality and horror."*

These words of a Bible scholar describe Jehu's rise to power as depicted in the ninth and tenth chapters of 2 Kings—yet how easily could they be the words of a contemporary historian applied to Hitler.

As more and more question marks arose about Hitler's rise to power, a question was asked in a subsequent world affairs reading of 1935.

Q–4. Explain the relation between the information just given regarding Germany and the changes for this year, and the information already given through this channel on Hitler.
A–4. Read that, my children, that has been given; that there was the destiny for the man, if he did not allow imperialism to enter in— and it is entering. Hence must be called into question. (3976–15)

---

*Interpreter's Bible, Abingdon Press.

Was Jehu psychically developed as the readings imply Hitler was? If so, then both men were open to a deeper source of unconscious vitality, energy and charisma which made them "chosen" leaders. They were subjective channels of a higher force. How they used—or allowed that energy to be used—becomes the personal responsibility of that soul.

Q-7. Why is it that apparently Hitler is making a mistake in initiating policies that seem to be antagonizing the world? (4 Nov. 1933)
A-7. Because the world has as yet not understood wholly Hitler's policies. For these are initiated rather from the spiritual source; and the world is very material-minded, and oft understands little of spiritual direction or dictation. But they must come to understand, unless there is more injection of the imperialistic influences . . . (3976-13)

A destiny called into question—*the corruption of a call.*

If Cayce's clairvoyance is trustworthy, at some point between 1933 and 1934, the time between the two world affairs readings 3976-13 and 3976-15, Hitler's "call" became irrevocably corrupted as "imperialistic" forces rather than his own psychic, or "inner" guidance began to dictate his policies.

Hitler was presented with choices between spiritual direction and imperialism, and did not overcome the temptations to abuse and misuse the power that his guidance delivered to him. If pure religious motivation was detected by Elijah and Elisha in Jehu, it, too, became corrupted in his bloody rise to power. What Jehu's obstacles and stumbling blocks were, we don't know. We only know his heart was not pure in the Lord, and, as king of Israel, he "walked in the ways of Jeroboam, which made Israel sin."

It is a challenging task to rethink our position on

Hitler to include the view taken toward him in the readings—as difficult as it has been for generations of Bible scholars who have had to reconcile Jehu's methods with God's plan.

Although we can't know the inner-condition of the heart and soul of these two dictators, we do have a means of judging. "By their fruits ye shall know them." Hitler's legacy bespeaks the darkness of the imperialism which possessed him. Jehu fulfilled, in part, the purpose for which he had been called, but did not remain loyal to the spirit which had raised him.

And so it is written of him:

Thus Jehu wiped out Baal from Israel. But Jehu did not turn aside from the sins of Jeroboam the son of Nebat, which he made Israel to sin, the golden calves that were in Bethel and in Dan. And the Lord said to Jehu, "Because you have done well in carrying out what is right in my eyes, and have done to the house of Ahab, according to all that was in my heart, your sons of the fourth generation shall sit on the throne of Israel."

But Jehu was not careful to walk in the law of the Lord God of Israel with all his heart; he did not turn from the sins of Jeroboam, which he made Israel to sin. (2 Kings 10:28–31)

THE GREAT TRIBULATION—CYCLES AND PATTERNS AND PROPHECY FULFILLED

Jehu was raised as the fulfillment of a prophecy —to complete the destruction destined for Ahab's house, and to purge Israel of Baalism—a religion all too frequently attractive to the Israelites. Perhaps, in the Old Testament sense, Hitler was also raised as a "rod of chastisement" who, possessed by the power given to him, went too far.

How difficult it is for us to fathom the working of

spiritual forces as they manifest through the physical and mental expressions of men. There is ever-present in the story of man the Old Testament necessity of purging and cleansing until the conditions laid down in the first commandment can be met—the unqualified and universal love for God, neighbor, and self.

Q-1. Analyze Hitler's attitude toward the Jews. (November 4, 1933)*
A-1. When the *character* of those that have received, in a manner, their dictations—or the dictates of the activity of the director in affairs—is considered, then it will be understood how that this is but that dictation which was given of old; and how that those peoples though they *were* called—have wandered far afield, and their rebelliousness and their seeking into the affairs of *others* has rather brought *them* into *their* present position.

Read they not that which has been given? "When ye forsake my ways ye shall be scattered, ye shall be without those things that would bring ye into the knowledge—until that time is fulfilled."

---

*In 1878, Rabbi Hile Weschler wrote these words of warning: "Although there were enemies of the Jews at all times, it is our time which has created an anti-Semitism of a thoroughness which has never existed before . . . One wants to destroy the Semitic element lock, stock and barrel . . . and ruin the Jews so radically that their atoms will never be connected and resynthesized."

After twelve years of Nazidom, these words are not surprising—but written sixty years before Hitler, they are genuinely clairvoyant. (See *The Reluctant Prophet*, by James Kirsch, Sherbourne Press, Los Angeles, 1973, Ch. 4.)

Rabbi Weschler's analysis of the cause—the Jews' own spiritual apathy—and the purpose of the tribulation—to accelerate the advent of the Messiah—agrees in intent with Cayce's interpretation in 1933 of "Hitler's attitude toward the Jews," as given above.

Clearly the law as perceived by Moses (Deut. 31:16-21) and later by Jeremiah is still in effect, as it ever will be.

Hence that attitude that is assumed is rather a fulfillment of that prophecy that has been made, and is the beginning of the return that must come throughout the earth. (3976–13)

A LESSON ON POWER

What a warning and lesson should Hitler—and others, such as Jehu and Jeroboam—be to those who seek material power to implement their ideals.

A warning was given to a group of men who saw in Edgar Cayce an unparalleled opportunity to use his psychic capacities to form and guide a world organization to "control finance, railroads, oil and steel industries, newspaper and news syndicates and shipping industries," using the "power and influence gained thereby . . . for the upbuilding of mankind." In a sense, to establish "The Kingdom of God" on earth.

The warning on power given here not only applies to the lessons of the Bible, but embraces all souls of all religions in every nation in all of time.

A lesson is given here:

> . . . such conditions have been the dream of many an individual; and of many with much more material power and prestige than those as would consider such at the present. Same was the idea of Alexander when he sought to conquer the world, yet the tenets of the ideal were forgotten in the desires of the flesh, and while the principles as set forth in the mind and heart of the man as the student under Plato and Archimedes, and Aurelius and others, the *man* became so gorged by the greed of power as to become the loathsome body—as it passed to its reward for the use of the power as given into the hands. (3976–4) (February 11, 1927)

Idealism may direct the mind of a leader to the source of power within and give the words and concepts which inspire many to follow—but what happens when one accedes to power and temptations multiply? How difficult it is to be a David, and how few there are in the world—and only one Christ in history! Or, as has been said, elsewhere, "what does it profit a man to gain the whole world, and lose his own soul?"

JOASH

The Halfway King
(2 Kings 11, 12; 2 Chronicles 22:11; 23; 24)

Joash did that "which was right" in God's sight "all the days of Jehoiadah, the priest," his guardian and protector.

Under Jehoiadah's guidance, Joash ordered the temple restored. A collection box was built through which donations were received to finance the project. The people were drawn back into the spiritual life of Judah by contributing to the temple restoration. Each person was called to do his part in strengthening and rebuilding the spirit of the nation. Their true defense was to always return to the original purpose for which the nation was brought into existence.

But after the death of Jehoiadah, egotism again showed itself in Judah. Joash permitted himself to be worshiped by the princes of Judah, thus turning them away from true spiritual worship. When Zedekiah, Jehoiadah's son, censured Joash, Joash had him killed.

Judah began to get a forecast of the great tribulation ahead, as their spiritual unity began to ebb. Joash's grandfather, Jehoshaphat, was a king and spiritual leader. With a small army he had defied "a million Ethiopians." (2 Chronicles 14) With Joash, conditions were reversed. Hazael of Damascus came against Joash's troops with a small army and was victorious. (2 Chronicles 24:24) Joash lacked the spiritual attunement within which insures victory, but he did possess the gold and holy things which had been brought to the temple. Joash turned Hazael away with the hallowed objects of the temple and gold from the treasury paid as tribute.

Joash was assassinated by his own servants, as an act of revenge for Zedekiah.

Although Judah made a continuous effort to keep the Spirit alive, there was never the ability to put aside "the sins of Solomon." Selfish instincts, material gain, and lack of vision were never completely cleansed from the national spirit, and Judah drifted into a decline.

During Joash's reign, Joel prophesied. He foresaw the impending disasters, but also beyond, to the end of the bitter cycle, and gave Israel (or man) one of its great assurances.

> *"And it shall come to pass afterward that I will pour out my spirit upon all flesh; and your sons and your daughters shall prophesy, your old men shall dream dreams, your young men shall see visions; and also upon the servants and the handmaids in those days will I pour out my spirit."* *(Joel 2:28)*

Both kingdoms faced dark days, unrelieved by any hope except through those who trusted God and were preparing for the coming judgment. In Cayce's day, the same "latter day" cycle of tribulation leading to purification was building. We find in a world affairs reading Joel's prophecy as counsel to those who were to pass through the dark night of world crisis:

> Thus it will require—yea, demand—that there be an expression on the part of each as to that given 3,200 years ago: "Declare ye today WHOM ye will serve! As for me and my house, we will serve a living God."

If there is sufficient, then, of those that will not only declare this in mind and in purpose but by deed and word of mouth, there may come then an enlightening through that which has been promised of old; that the young men shall dream dreams, the old men shall have visions, the daughters or maidens may know the spirit of truth—yea, that all may come to the greater knowledge of the indwelling of the Prince of Peace. (3976–26)

5

New Light

UZZIAH

When Amaziah became king, he slew his father's assassins, but permitted their children to live, thus honoring the law of Moses which said that every man should suffer for his own sins, and not the children for the sins of their parents, or the parents for their children's sins. Amaziah listened to those prophets who stressed a literal application of the law. Amaziah did "what was right in the sight of the Lord" but "not with a perfect heart."

Joash and Amaziah were basically good kings, sufficiently aware of spiritual forces, yet not stable in their ideals. Thus, through their reigns, Judah kept sliding into a decline.

However, King Uzziah renewed the light and drew the people back to God. He did that "which was right" in the sight of God, "according to all that his father David did." "He prayed before the Lord" and was the student of Zechariah, priest and prophet, who instructed Uzziah "in the worship of the Lord."

The fact the Biblical writer recorded that Uzziah was a student of Zechariah indicates that it was noteworthy and important. Ritualistic worship dates back to the days of Moses. (Jethro, Moses' father-in-law, was adept in ritual sacrifice: see 1266–1.) Through sacred ritual, the initiates in the priesthood could attune to higher dimensions of the spirit, or soul-forces, and manifest greater degrees of psychic energy and consciousness than ordinarily possessed by man.

Uzziah must have been an able student. He conquered the Philistines and the Arabians, and received tribute from the Ammonites. He refortified his country, reorganized and re-equipped his army, and personally engaged in agricultural pursuits. His success as king and commander-in-chief made him the ruler over the largest realm in Judah since the disruption of the kingdom.

Yet his strength became his weakness. Uzziah must have been sufficiently impressed with the office of the priesthood and the knowledge of Zechariah to want to be a priest himself as well as king. Uzziah usurped the privileges of the priesthood, and judgment was swift. While burning incense at the altar, Uzziah was struck with leprosy and forced to live his last years in a leper's house.

Cayce philosophized with the Bible class on this point:

> "Why do people today who blaspheme God's word, or do wicked things, not meet their punishment as suddenly as many of those who were in authority at that time? They were in that stage of evolution where quick judgments came. Then it was 'an eye for an eye, a tooth for a tooth.' Today, though we may not agree with it or look at it this way, because of Christ's advent into the world, God is more merciful. We are under the law of mercy and not judgment. Our punishment is longer in coming, but more severe in the end. When we are shown over and over again, and still sin against the Holy Spirit,

there's no forgiving, there's no getting around the law of cause and effect.

"In the olden days, they were quick to pass judgment on themselves—so judgments came quickly. This is a thought concerning it, at least."

JOTHAM AND THE PROPHETIC VOICE

Jotham ruled during Uzziah's confinement as a leper, and succeeded him after his death. The year King Uzziah died, a momentous event took place, the effects of which are still reverberating on the skein of time and space—Isaiah achieved a cosmic awareness and, baptized by the Spirit, began his ministry. (Isaiah 6)

Personal spiritual experiences are perhaps the most profound and overlooked factors shaping and molding man's history. The quiet corners where individuals meditate, or a bed where revelation or guidance has been received through a dream, has been the place where many of the great movements and institutions which have affected our destiny have begun.

Or, as one reading tells us:

The beginning of all great institutions, of all great things, is first in the mind of individuals who are in touch with infinite forces. (254–31)

The Bible itself, another reading tells us, is the greatest collection of psychic experiences in the world. Not only does it describe a variety of phenomena, but also tells what individuals did about their experiences. The Bible is a witness to the worth of the individual spiritual experience, and its cumulative value when it is lived and applied. Abraham was only a merchant's son until he heard a voice and acted on it. Isaiah would have been soon forgotten if, as the cousin of Uzziah and grandson of Joash, he had valued only his royal blood and not his soul.

Many names remain with us from this period because of their spiritual beliefs and actions. The prophetic voice was rising in Judah and Israel, and with it came a new tension and struggle. It was the conflict between priest and prophet. Internalized, it represents the struggle within self between intellect and intuition.

Jotham did right like his father, but did not remove all the high places. He inherited a strong government and defeated the Ammonites, who paid him immense annual tribute. But the increasing corruption of the north kingdom began permeating Judah, as seen in the words of Isaiah and Micah. Hosea refers to Judah under Jotham as lacking in purity of life and worship.

AHAZ

Ahaz followed Jotham. Cayce described him to the Bible class:

> "Ahaz started out right, with high ideals and purposes; but, like so many, his environment got the best of him."

Ahaz yielded to the glamour and prestige of the Assyrians in religion and politics.

When Pekah, a murderer and usurper and eighteenth of the nineteen kings of the north kingdom, appealed to Ahaz to join him and the Syrian king in a league against Assyria, Ahaz turned to Assyria for help. He stripped the temple of all the silver and gold and sent it as a present to the mighty Tiglath-pileser III, who was preparing to attack Palestine and Syria. Tiglath-pileser accepted, and did not invade Judah, and relieved Ahaz of his troublesome neighbors, Israel and Syria.

Ahaz journeyed to Damascus and swore homage to the Assyrian king and his gods. When he returned to Jerusalem, Ahaz rearranged the temple trappings and the services to comform to Assyrian standards.

However, Assyria had an enormous appetite. Tiglath-pileser was not content with one payment from Ahaz, but returned and demanded—or extorted—more and more tribute. The payments drained Judah of its resources, and Ahaz' policies, which were influenced by his weaknesses, fears, and lack of faith, took the people farther and farther from the true understanding of the Spirit. His policies were strongly opposed by Isaiah, who counseled the king to rely upon God. But Ahaz could not find it within himself to do so.

Cayce made a summary of Ahaz' reign. He told the class:

> "On the whole, Ahaz' government was disas-
> trous to his country, especially in its religious
> aspects, which is—or should be—the main
> consideration in every country. When there is
> a decline in the religion of a country, a de-
> cline in political power soon follows, although
> it may appear to prosper in a greater measure
> for a short time.
>
> "When we come to Hezekiah, Ahaz' son,
> we will see that a large part of his reforming
> work was aimed at undoing the evil Ahaz had
> wrought."

Ahaz' manipulations with Assyria yielded immediate blessings, but inwardly, his policies worked a
greater curse. They led to a continued deterioration of
the kingdom, and proved what all man's political, military, and economic maneuvers do—that God is not
mocked!

An interpretation in a world affairs reading strikes
this note about a contemporary situation (June, 1939).

> Then ye ask, "What is to be the outcome
> of England and France in their efforts to join
> hands with Russia as an encirclement of the
> totalitarian regime?" These, so long as they
> are in keeping with God's purposes with man,

will succeed. When they become active for self-preservation without the thought or purpose of their fellow man, they must fail.

So it is with the endeavors of Germany, Italy, Japan. As they attempt to preserve their own personalities, their own selves, without thought of their fellow man, they may succeed for the moment, but "God is not mocked," and whatsoever a man, a country, a nation sows, that it must reap . . .

Then, rest not on those things that become as quicksand about thee, but on the true, the tried arm of God. For the earth is His, and the fullness thereof. (3976–23)

6

Good King Hezekiah

King Hezekiah is best known for his moral and spiritual leadership, and for his association with the prophet Isaiah. Under his reign, Judah returned briefly to a pure form of worship, based upon the prophetic guidance of Isaiah. Isaiah's visionary policies were, in the main, adhered to by King Hezekiah in matters of state. Jeremiah records Hezekiah listened to Micah as well. (Jeremiah 26:18, 19)

These were days of great upheaval and stress in Israel and Judah. Hezekiah saw Israel swept away by the Assyrians who ravaged the land and ordered the mass deportation of its people. While Hezekiah was king, tens of thousands of Israelites were violently taken from their homeland and resettled in foreign lands, and their places filled with conquered peoples from other areas. This was Assyrian policy, and its intent was to distroy national consciousness and break the will of the people.

With the exception of Samaria, all Israel was under Assyrian control. Nine years later Samaria was taken. Hezekiah, too, lost part of his kingdom to the Assyrians. He was a tribute paying vassal because his father, Ahaz, had voluntarily submitted to Tiglath-pileser.

In these darkest days, Hezekiah was a great light —for he "trusted in God" so that "after him there was

95

not one like him among all the kings of Judah nor among those who went before him." He did that which was right, just as his father David had done. (2 Chronicles 29:2) "He held fast to the Lord and turned not aside." (2 Kings 18:5, 6)

In a deteriorated kingdom, Hezekiah returned to the one tried and true defense—spiritual reform.

Hezekiah's first act as king was to order the repair of the temple, which had been closed during the reign of Ahaz. He reorganized the services of the priests and Levites, and cleansed the house of the Lord and all the vessels in it, which had been thrown away, purifying them. When everything was sanctified and set in order, Hezekiah gathered the rulers of the city and went to offer sacrifice. A sin offering was made, the sins of the people were rolled back through the releasing of the scapegoat. Offerings were made while the people sang praises to the Lord and worshiped. The offerings were so abundant the priests had to ask the Levites for help.

Hezekiah rejoiced with his people—the Lord had preserved them, the house of the Lord was in order!

Hezekiah's effort, with Isaiah, was to center the collective consciousness of the people on the Lord.

Cayce told his class:

"Hezekiah was a righteous man and knew the wrath of the Lord would not be turned from Judah until the people turned again to God."

The temple was the great binding focus between the people and God. Hezekiah's next step was to involve the people of both kingdoms in his reforms and renewals. He sent messengers throughout Israel and Judah, asking the people to come to Jerusalem to keep the Passover. The Passover had not been observed on this scale for many years. News of its revival brought scorn and mockery by some, but many people responded. A great crowd gathered, and the Passover was celebrated with great solemnity and rejoicing as had not been seen since Solomon's days.

The crowd which assembled for the Passover was so large the priests could not minister to them. And many of the people ate the Passover feast who had not been cleansed according to Mosaic law.

The need for the Passover was greater than the need to observe the law. The situation led—or forced—Hezekiah to trust a spiritual intuition: that the spirit was greater than the law.

When Hezekiah saw the Passover was violating the ritual law, he prayed beautifully:

"Lord, pardon everyone that prepares his heart to seek God, the Lord God of his fathers, though he be not cleansed according to the purification of the sanctuary." (2 Chronicles 30:18)

Thus he added to an evolving consciousness.

This same prophetic understanding is shown by Samuel, when he rebuked Saul: "To obey is better than to sacrifice, to harken better than burnt offerings." (1 Samuel 15:22)

This same counsel Cayce offered the nation in a world affairs reading of 1939:

Then, there needs be that not so much be set as to this ritual, or this form, or the other, for any given peoples or any nation, but rather that the individuals in each nation, EVERY-WHERE, are to turn again TO the God of the fathers and not in self-indulgence, self-aggrandizement, but more and more of self-effacement.

For as the people of each nation pray, AND then live that prayer, so must the Spirit work. (3976–23)

In an interesting life reading for a Russian jeweler who had been a craftsman who worked on the restoration of the temple for Hezekiah, we find the same counsel regarding spiritual understanding.

Before that we find the entity was in the land now known as the Promised Land, during that particular period of Hezekiah, the king in Judah, who opened again the house of the Lord of those peoples.

And the entity—as Jabin—was a worker in metals; being among those peoples given the privilege and authority (notice those words) to restore the utensils pertaining to the worship, and the activities especially in the courts of the temple; restoring the censers upon which incense was burned.

Hence, in the present there are not only the abilities to work in metals—as of gold, silver, brass and the like—but the knowledge of the value to bestow upon odors, and certain activities pertaining to the burning of incense . . .

As were the promptings of those activities directed by the entity in that sojourn as Jabin, know that the intent and purpose must be for the worship of—because of the faith in, and the promptings of the heart and mind and soul—toward—a living God! Not alone to reach a certain effect, through affecting certain poses or conditions in the relationships and activities of self toward others, or the prompting of others as to shortcuts to attain certain results in their material affairs.

To be sure, the law is, "They that receive a prophet in the name of a prophet, receive the prophet's reward." Yet, as indicated in that given above, both may fall in the ditch and be far, far from living and being wholly

acceptable unto Him, who IS the Giver of all
good and perfect gifts! (2077–1)

The Passover celebration drew the people together
into one body as they had not been since David's time.
After the feast, they went out and broke down the images and cut down the groves and smashed the altars on
the high places. The whole nation was seeking for God
as one people.

Their unity was necessary, for the people were
soon called to face the awesome threat of Assyria.

Hezekiah had been successful in his wars against
the Philistines, driving them back as far as Gaza. He
retook all the cities lost by his father and conquered
others belonging to the Philistines. Hezekiah was aided
in his campaign by Isaiah, upon whose prophecies he
relied, venturing even to revolt against Assyria by refusing to pay the usual tribute. Hezekiah came under
Isaiah's influence only after a hard struggle with certain ministers, who advised him to enter into an alliance
with Egypt. The alliance was not acceptable to Isaiah.
He saw it as a deviation from trust in God. He advised
Hezekiah to rely upon God and no one else.

Eight years after the fall of Samaria and the mass
deportation of the Israelites, the fourteenth year of
Hezekiah's reign, Assyria marched against Judah, con-
quering many cities.

An Assyrian victory monument bears this inscrip-
tion: "Sennacherib captured 46 strong cities and carried
away captive into Assyria, 200,150 captives of the men
of Judah."

When Sennacherib invaded, Hezekiah lost his
faith. He acknowledged his fault (in not paying tribute)
and parleyed with Sennacherib for a new treaty. The
Assyrian imposed a new levy of three hundred talents
of silver and thirty of gold. Hezekiah was forced to take
all the silver in the temple and from his own treasury
to pay it, even to "cut off the gold from the doors of
the temple."

After receiving the tribute, Sennacherib sent a large army under three of his generals to besiege Jerusalem. Rahshakeh, the leader, called upon Hezekiah to surrender. He mocked Hezekiah for his hope in Egypt and made an effort to inspire the people with mistrust in Hezekiah's reliance upon God.

This disastrous turn of events must have turned Hezekiah back to God, or made him realize there was no hope or help except from God. In this trial, Hezekiah kept the faith. He took the letters with the Assyrian terms to the temple and laid them open before the Lord and prayed for the deliverance of Jerusalem.

While Hezekiah poured out his soul in the temple, Isaiah received God's word and carried it to the king. Sennacherib would not invade, Isaiah promised, but would be forced to return "by the way that he came" and would not trouble Jerusalem again. (2 Kings 19)

Isaiah's prophecy was quick to be confirmed. Sennacherib was forced to withdraw because the king of Ethiopia was marching against him. That night, the "angel of death," through the agency of a plague or an infection, destroyed the whole Assyrian army. Sennacherib returned home in shame and was murdered by his own sons while praying in the house of his gods.

The threat passed. Judah was released for the time being, and, relieved and inspired, they gave all the credit to God.

"THEY WERE THERE"

The cruelty of the Assyrians is legendary. However, in this life reading we find one with a quality of mercy.

A reading for a young society matron mentions Sennacherib and places the entity among the Assyrian royalty.

> . . . we find the entity was in the land now known as the Persian, when there was the

arousing of the peoples for the influences which were a part of that experience in the land when Sennacherib and the peoples were overcoming the Jewish forces.

There we find the entity was among those of the household then of the ruling forces—or of the ruler himself.

Hence we find those things of pomp, of power, of wealth, of all the activities that went with the period, were a part of the entity's experience.

The name then was Shedeli. In the experience the entity gained, for the entity showed mercy to those who were under the entity in the periods when the helpmeet and those of the entity's people became rulers over those of the land.

And in the present it may be said that this was one of the greater virtues—the patience the entity has with those who are in a more menial position, or who are in the social status beneath the entity's position. (1752–1)

In this reading, Cayce described for a Jewish girl her experience as an Assyrian captive:

. . . we find the entity was in the land during the reign of Hezekiah, when the peoples of promise were taken into captivity.

There we find the entity was under the material hardships, and forgot not its own tenets and teachings that were given in the early part of its activities in the holy city and its environs there.

Thus, in the name Vistula, the entity's activities in those new environs, new scenes, among new faces and new activities, brought great experiences of development.

Yet little hates, petty malices, the desire for freedom, arise from these experiences.

One may be free indeed in thought, though the body may be bound in chains; and be much more free than those who are chained by their own consciousness in those things which are in keeping with the ideals in the material as well as mental and spiritual life.

These understandings the entity must gain through the abilities to curb self, in being too quickly outspoken when little resentments arise. For this once gained, the entity may again come to know much of those experiences that were gained even in the lands where foreign activities, foreign associations, foreign purposes, even foreign worship in the spiritual things, were roundabout—yet the heart kept singing all the while the purposes of the living God.

And these should be aroused, and held to—"Let others do as they may, but as for me and mine, we will serve a living God." Let these be as frontlets upon thine eyes, as those influences upon thine hands—yea, as that above all that would govern thy speech and thy activity! Thus ye will find that peace, that harmony, which is beyond price—and may indeed be called blessed by many!

For then ye *live,* rather than just profess, thy relationships to thy Maker! (1669–1)

A Pennsylvania man was told he had been one of Hezekiah's soldiers taken as hostage by Assyria—and found God!

Before that the entity was in the Holy Land, when those activities were being broken up by the order of the king when the people had so belittled themselves by gratifying their own selfish desires and had forgotten the ways of the Lord; and, as the warnings had been given, they were carried away into captivity.

The entity was among those of the soldiery at the time of Benaiah, when the soldiery of Hezekiah was carried away.

In the foreign land the entity remembered. Hence in the present there are the periods when the entity becomes retrospective and it brings discomforts, yet a joy. For ye will still recall that the promise is, "Though ye be far away, if ye call I will hear."

Then turn ye to Exodus 19:5 and begin —and find self. Then turn to Deuteronomy 4 and again read those warnings that are a part of thy experience from that sojourn, and a part of thine own headstrongness in the present.

From that experience the entity learned to write. For, as Benaiah, the entity was educated in the schools of those lands where the entity was taken as hostage. (3528–1)

HEZEKIAH, FIGS AND BABYLON

During the Assyrian siege, Hezekiah fell dangerously ill with Job's affliction—boils—which Isaiah diagnosed as fatal. All illness comes from sin, the readings tell us, and Hezekiah's was due "to the pride of his heart." (2 Chronicles 32:25)

Hezekiah wept bitterly and prayed earnestly to live, reminding God how righteously he had lived "before pride exalted his heart." As Hezekiah poured out his soul in prayer, Isaiah heard the answer as he walked through the temple courts. Hezekiah had fifteen years added to his life because of the sincerity of his prayer. Perhaps Isaiah was even given guidance on the cure—a fig poultice, which he applied to Hezekiah's boils, and the king recovered.

Those who are familiar with the Cayce readings are aware of the efficacy of his "home remedies" and the variety of poultices he prescribed, which include everything from grapes and onions to castor oil and turpentine—all of which have amazing healing properties when applied in right combinations to specific illnesses. A poultice of figs and warm milk was recommended a few times for gum and tooth infections. Apparently it was an old remedy used in dentistry. An ancient manual of veterinary science dating from 1500 B.C. recommends a fig poultice for horses suffering with swollen heads and sore noses. The healing properties in figs for combating certain types of infection were recognized by people in the ancient orient, and used by Isaiah to cure Hezekiah.*

Many of Cayce's remedies are as ancient as man, dating back to Biblical times and beyond, and, like Isaiah's poultice, consist entirely of ingredients supplied by nature.

But these external means are only aids and not the source of healing. According to the readings, the healing must come from within. The outward means—whether physical, mental, or spiritual—act only to stimulate, awaken and coordinate with the individual's own latent healing forces. Cayce made a cogent perception on Hezekiah's recovery. He told his students:

> "Hezekiah was cured of his boils by a poultice of figs. No doubt the infection was spreading, and the poultice was necessary—but the spiritual seeking and awakening had to come first."

---

*Werner Keller, *The Bible as History*.

The kingdom of Israel was destroyed by Assyria, and Judah fell to the Babylonians over a century later. Assyrian dominance continued for another eighty years after the death of Sennacherib until the brutal empire, beset by Scythians, Medes, and Babylonians, fell and Babylon gained mastery. Isaiah had the first clear insight in the Babylonian ascendancy years before it happened, and knew what it held in store for Judah.

The first mention of Babylon in the Bible, an advance notice of the future history, is contained in the story of Hezekiah's sickness.

After his recovery, the king of Babylon sent ambassadors to Hezekiah to congratulate him on his return to health and to inquire about the miracle. The real purpose for the visit was to ascertain if an alliance with Judah would be advantageous for his own kingdom in his struggle against Assyria.

Hezekiah received the Babylonians eagerly and escorted them through his temple, the palace, and the armory. Hezekiah showed the ambassadors that he was a man of great importance and not to be despised. His boils had been healed, but his "pride" had not. The lesson had been forgotten.

Isaiah rebuked Hezekiah. He read in the king's behavior a distrust in divine power. Hezekiah repented, but it was not enough to turn aside that which Isaiah had foreseen.

> Then Isaiah said to Hezekiah, Hear the word of the Lord. Behold, the days are coming when all that is in your house and that which your fathers have laid up in treasure to this day shall be carried to Babylon; nothing shall be left for you, says the Lord.
>
> And of your sons that shall issue from you,

whom you shall beget, shall they take away; and they shall be eunuchs in the palace of the kings of Babylon. (2 Kings 20:16–18)

Was this punishment for Hezekiah's sin—or a condition which had been steadily building because Judah continually wavered between trust in God, and looking to outside forces for support? Judah's decline into captivity and servitude could have been avoided had the people and leaders looked steadily to God and followed the inner guidance of the still, small voice which is so easily overlooked amid the emotional upheavals of the day. Hezekiah, although a great example of a God-trusting man, allowed "external" events to alter his vision. Few of his descendants even matched his development, and all—until Christ—remained in that state of consciousness—and confusion—of wavering between turning within and looking without, a state of mind we find ourselves still in today.

THE GROWING DARKNESS

Manassah and Amon

When Hezekiah fell ill, he was without an heir. The Davidic dynasty was again in danger.

During the fifteen years which were added to his life, Hezekiah's son, Manassah was born. Manassah had the longest reign of any of the kings of Judah, and it is considered the most wicked. He spurred a reaction to Hezekiah's reforms and reintroduced all the pagan cultic worship. The Assyrians regarded Judah as a conquered and tribute-paying province, and in their inscriptions refer to Manassah as a vassal king.

According to Chronicles, Manassah was brought in chains to Babylon by the king of Assyria, where he repented and was restored by God to his throne. But in Kings nothing is said of his change of heart, rather three deplorable details of his reign are stressed: the free adoption of foreign cults, the religious reaction which followed his reign, and the bitter persecution of the prophets.

Amon, Manassah's son, was twenty-two years old when he began his reign and ruled two years, following in his father's footsteps. "Amon forsook the Lord and followed not in the ways of the Lord." Though he ruled in a critical time, little is known of his reign.

If the story is true in Chronicles about Manassah's repentance in Babylon, the lesson was lost on Amon. Manassah humbled himself, acknowledged that the Lord was God, and prayed to return to Jerusalem. When he did, he led a different life. He built a wall about the city of David, removed the strange gods, repaired the altars in the house of the Lord, offered sacrifices, and commanded Judah to serve the living God.

Cayce commented on Amon to the Bible class:

> "Evidently the lesson his father learned did Amon no good. He was about seventeen years old when Manassah experienced his change of heart, and this is a hard lesson to learn by observation. Amon trespassed more and more until his servants conspired and slew him, and made Josiah king."

The endeavors of the prophets to establish a pure form of religion were, for a short time, successful under Hezekiah; but a reaction set in after Hezekiah's death. Both Amon and Manassah followed the popular trend in re-establishing the old Canaanite cults. For many decades, those who sympathized with prophetic ideas were in constant danger.

THE LAST GREAT LIGHT

Josiah

Josiah was eight years old when he became king, and ruled thirty-one years. He did that which was right and walked in the ways of David, turning "neither to the left nor right." (2 Kings 22:2)

Three momentous events occurred under Josiah: Jeremiah began to prophesy; lost books of the Law of Moses were discovered; and Josiah inaugurated the great reformation which marks an epoch in the religious history of Israel, and insured the preservation of a remnant:

> . . . yet only in Josiah was it given to again approach even the threshold of the understanding as was necessary for the deliverance of a portion of the peoples, even sufficient to keep the natural lineage of the promised one. (900–428)

In his eighth year, Josiah began to seek God, and in his twelfth, he purged Judah of the images, groves, and high places. In his thirteenth, Jeremiah began to receive the word of God and had the vision concerning his purpose. (Jeremiah 1) In his eighteenth year, Josiah began repairing the house of the Lord, and the book of the law was found. Josiah became greatly alarmed that the calamities (2 Chronicles 34) threatened in the law for non-observance of its commands, would come upon him and his people. This inspired the great reformation.

Solomon's example of tolerance to pagan practices, and his stress on luxury and privilege, created deteriorating inroads and were blinding to man's spiritual consciousness. Despite the determined efforts of the good kings and inspired prophets, the persistent stain of selfish desires and evil purposes in the national moral and spiritual fabric would not be cleansed. Asa, Jehoshaphat, Uzziah, and Hezekiah, and prophets like Elijah, Elisha, Isaiah and Jeremiah kept the knowledge of the spirit from being lost entirely. By giving evidence of the effect of the Spirit in their lives, they advanced the consciousness.

Without them, there would not have been the hope, the fortitude, and the inspiration to encourage Judah to place its faith in an unseen force, a spirit that "did not think like men," yet had promised through David an eternal throne and a future king. The history of Judah shows a consistent and continuous effort to keep this spirit and understanding alive.

In Josiah's time, the effort bore fruit. The understanding was preserved, insuring that there would be a remnant with enough devotion and conviction of the spirit to pass down their understanding through the next one hundred years of national trauma, captivity, deportation and servitude.

THE COUNTDOWN BEGINS

The Last Kings

Following the death of Josiah, Judah's decline was rapid. The people anointed Jehoahaz to replace his father. Jehoahaz was not first in the order of succession, but popular with the people. Perhaps, as Edgar Cayce suggested, he was the most likely spiritual successor to his father.

His reign was brief—three months. Necho, pharaoh of Egypt, invaded Judah and carried him captive, never to return. Necho installed Eliakim, Jehoahaz' elder brother, on the throne, and changed his name to Jehoiakim. Judah was under Egyptian domination and paid a heavy tribute.

Nebuchadnezzar invaded Palestine, entered Jerusalem, and compelled Jehoiakim to pay tribute to Babylon. After three years, Jehoiakim rebelled and Nebuchadnezzar returned, and took Jehoiakim back to Babylon in chains and fetters.

Jehoiakim died after an evil reign of eleven years. It was he who slew the prophet Uriah "and cast his dead body into the graves of the common people." (Jeremiah 26) Jehoiakim was also the king who impiously destroyed Jeremiah's scroll of prophecies and threw it into the fire as it was being read to him. (Jeremiah 36)

Jehoiakim was so despised by his people that when he died he was buried "with the burial of an ass, drawn, and cast forth beyond the gates of Jerusalem." (Jeremiah 22:19)

Jehoiakim's son, Jehoiachin, reigned only three months. He was scarcely on the throne when Nebuchadnezzar returned and took him, his mother, his servants, captains, and officers captive and sent them to Babylon. The treasures of the palace and the sacred vessels of the temple were taken also. Jehoiachin remained in prison in Babylon for thirty-six years. When Nebuchadnezzar died, his son Evil-merodach released Jehoiachin and gave him an honorable seat at his table.

Nebuchadnezzar gave Jehoiachin's crown to Mattaniah (son of Josiah), whose name was changed to Zedekiah.

Zedekiah was the last king of Judah and the youngest son of Josiah. He was a full brother to Jehoahaz, who was carried captive to Egypt by Necho.

The eleven years of Zedekiah's reign are notable for the steady decline in Judah's power, and for the desperate efforts of Jeremiah to avert the coming disaster.

Zedekiah was a weak king, pliant and yielding readily to the influence of any advisor, whether prince or prophet. At times he would listen to Jeremiah, and at others follow counsel that was in direct opposition.

In the fourth year of his reign he journeyed to Babylon to swear an oath of allegiance to Nebuchadnezzar. But the Egyptian king persuaded Zedekiah to break his oath.

Zedekiah rebelled, in spite of Jeremiah's counsel to submit to the inevitable "yoke of slavery" as the judgment of God and a lesson to be learned. The revolt brought the Babylonian army back to Jerusalem.

Jerusalem was taken, plundered, and burned; its best population deported to Babylon as captives. As a result of his conspiracies and as punishment for his rebellion, all Zedekiah's heirs to the throne were slain before his eyes, then he was blinded and taken to Babylon as a rebel prisoner.

The Jewish kingdom perished. Israel ceased to exist as an independent nation. Zedekiah lived out the rest of his life in a Babylonian dungeon.

Although Zedekiah's punishment was severe, Cayce gave a compensating view to the Bible class.

"It seems horrible that Zedekiah, although an evil king, should have to suffer, first by seeing his sons killed before his eyes, then his own eyes put out, and spending the rest of his days in a dungeon. Although no more evil than many of the other kings of Judah, he had a prolonged suffering, while many others 'got by' with a horrible but sudden death after a life lived in luxury.

"While it appears Zedekiah's was the greater punishment, and that sudden death would be easier—and more merciful—we can only judge from the outward appearance. God looks on the heart. Perhaps it took years and years for those other kings to become adjusted to their state after passing from this earth, or they may have had to pass through periods of suffering, as Dives in the parable of Dives and Lazarus. (Luke 16:19–31)

"Suffering in the material sense, such as Zedekiah's, can make us spiritually strong within. Zedekiah needed strength. He had been so wishy-washy throughout his reign. As the son of Josiah, he no doubt knew what was right from wrong, yet didn't have the courage of his convictions. Through his remaining years, though in a dungeon, he could review his life and build up strength for a nobler effort the next time he returned to earth.

"In other words, Zedekiah met his karma in that particular life, while some of the others did not."

7

The Lost Tribes and the New World

The kingdom of Israel fell over one hundred years before Zedekiah was taken to Babylon and Jerusalem destroyed. Judah had made a consistent effort to keep the Spirit alive, but could not overcome its own selfish spirit. Thus, the day of judgment was delayed, but not circumvented.

The people of both kingdoms continually disregarded the warnings of their prophets. The School of Prophets, begun by Samuel, and given its greatest impetus under Elijah, was turning out individuals familiar with higher states of consciousness and knowledgeable about the laws of cause and effect, or karma. The prophets knew how to "tune in" and receive from God. They were able to see the pattern in their people's choices and gain spiritual insights as to where it would lead.

The people were given opportunity after opportunity to reform, but did not. Instead of remaining true to the original inner convictions, they turned to the unrestricted and more sensually pleasant way of life they saw around them. Consequently they were ignoring divine law. Nothing could save them, but themselves.

They deliberately brought about their own destruction by rejecting God.

One of the rewards from the Cayce readings is to see new dimensions added to famous Bible characters, through actions which are unaccounted for in the Bible. When the north kingdom fell, the Israelites became victims to the cruel Assyrian policy of being violently driven from their homeland and deported to foreign lands. The aim of these uprooting tactics was clear: To destroy the sense of nationalism and to break the people's will to resist.

When the kings and people of the north kingdom were taken, they were absorbed into the population of foreign lands and never emerged again in history, and the fascinating question of "the lost tribes" arose. All investigation into what became of the ten tribes, until recently, has revealed nothing.

However, the Cayce readings indicate that King Hezekiah, under the guidance of Isaiah, may have given his support to a program of migrations and resettlements into parts of the world untouched by Assyrian power. And one of those lands was America!

In one reading, Cayce was asked:

Q-1. How did the lost tribe reach this country [America]?
A-1. In boats. (5750-1)

The lost tribes are being found. Although the question of where they went has never been settled, modern archeology is shedding new light on this old question, and the findings are supportive of statements made in the readings ten and twenty years earlier.*

Recent discoveries indicate the presence of Jewish voyagers to American soil several thousand years ago. This growing evidence confirms yet another unusual

---

*See Cyrus Gordon, Ph.D., *Before Columbus.*

chapter in Edgar Cayce's Story of the Old Testament and brings new insight to these statements by Isaiah:

> . . . the mighty men of the nations have broken down the branches . . . its shoots spread out, they are gone over the sea. (Isaiah 16:8)

> "I will set a sign among them, and those who escape I will send among the nations, to Tarshish, Pul, and Lud . . . To Tubal, and Javan, and to the islands afar off that have not heard my name."*
> (Isaiah 66:19)

When it became obvious that Assyria was the engine of destruction the prophets had foreseen, and its path of conquest could not be turned aside, the prophecies began to be taken more seriously. But for many, it was too late.

The ones who escaped were either the adventurous, or those with deep-seated spiritual motivations who felt a need to preserve their heritage and religion.

A young mathematics teacher was told in 1940 that she had been one of the adventurers:

> Before that the entity was in the English land, but during the early periods of those journeyings of the peoples of Hezekiah's reign —during the time when the children of promise were carried into captivity.
>
> The entity was among those voyagers who fared forth seeking out other lands.
>
> Hence the love of adventure, the love of strange places, strange environs; and the desire to study various activities when there may be indicated as to the source or cause of individuals thinking or acting in given directions.

---

*The locations of the places have never been determined.

Thus we find the abilities as the mathematician, or even the abilities as a nautical director; for the entity might easily have become either an aviatrix or one who would sail boats by the stars or by the compass or by those things considered rather as a MAN'S direction—though the entity has the more oft (in those sojourns that have an influence in the present experience) remained in its present sex.

The name then was Zenbeuen. In the experience the entity gained, for it was the seeking for freedom as well as for the preservation of those tenets and truths which brought the entity's desire to seek out other lands, and the putting of same into activity—and the setting up of the stones in the forms of circles for altars.

Hence we find that symbols at times mean much to the entity, or the study of same. (2205–1)

A young teen-ager was told in 1944 he had been a leader in the search for new land.

Before that the entity was in the land of the present nativity [United States] in the early periods when those came into this land from the separations or divisions of the peoples in the periods of uprisings in the Holy Land.

Then the entity was among the leaders in such activities.

Thus we will find activities of the unusual nature in the seeking out of strange places, strange things, will be a portion of the entity's innate and manifested nature. Don't let these wander too far afield (4084–1)

The readings describe two important Jewish colonies; one in England and another in the southwest United States. There are indications of a settlement in the South Seas (1253–1), in Peru (1159–1), and "the central portion of Ohio," during "the early period of the Mound Builders." (1286–1)

Other traditions would indicate other locations as well.

This extract describes the course of one migration:

> . . . during that period as would be called three thousand years before the Prince of Peace came, those peoples that were of the lost tribes, a portion came into the land; infusing their activities upon the peoples from Mu in the southernmost portion of that called America or United States, and then moved on to the activities in Mexico, Yucatan, centralizing that now about the spots where the central of Mexico now stands, or Mexico City. Hence there arose through the age a different civilization, a *mixture* again. (5750–1)

THE AMERICAN COLONY

The two following readings describe the colony in the American Southwest.

A reading for a Pennsylvania model and showgirl contains an important note about her purposes as a priestess in that spiritual center.

> Before that the entity was in the own land of nativity during the early settlings; not America as known in history, but when there were the activities of those peoples that were dispersed by the carrying away of the children of promise into captivity.
>
> The entity was among those born to

those who escaped across the waters into what is now the southwestern portion of the entity's present native land [America].

There the entity came in contact with those who were a part of the Atlantean civilization before it was broken up, and the entity was made a priestess—as in keeping with a combination of the old Mosaic teachings and those of Ax-Tell and the children of the Law of One.

The entity gained throughout the experience. For its purposes, its activities were not only for the betterment in the daily activity but for the building up of body and of mind by and through the application of spiritual laws that coordinate the physical manifestations in a material body.

The name then was Zes-Zeun. (2540-1)

A New Jersey librarian was told she had been among the newborn in the colony.

Before that the entity was again in the land of the present nativity during those periods when activities were set up or established in the Southwest, by those who had journeyed from other lands when the ten tribes were carried away.

The entity was among those children born in that land, now a portion of Arizona and New Mexico. These portions of the land appeal in many ways to the entity—the wide open spaces, and yet there is a desire for home, for security, in mental as well as in spiritual as may apply in material things.

The entity became a teacher, one after whom the young modeled, and things pertaining to such direction should be a part of the present experience of the entity. (3513-1)

Reading 4129, given in December, 1925, also mentions America, but no specific location is described.

> ... in the days when ... the peoples of the Promise came to the foreign shores in now America, the entity then ... came as the mother in the first of those peoples. Then in the name Ibeois, and the entity developed much in that plane and gained much spiritual understanding of the developments of people ... (4129–1)

THE ENGLISH COLONY

The most important center for the escaping Jews was in England. The site which drew them has a long history in the metaphysical and spiritual traditions of the world. The migration to England took the Jews to the legendary Druid center, the site of Stonehenge and future location of the first Christian church, settled in England by Joseph of Arimathaea in the first century, and later the fields of King Arthur's castle of the Holy Grail. This important spiritual center was active before the Jews arrived and has continued to exert a profound infleunce and mystery on man into the present. The readings enhance the legend.

Somerset is clearly described as the center where the royal family, the descendants of Hezekiah and Zedekiah, settled, joining with the children of Israel who had foregathered. The connection between Stonehenge and the altars built by the Jews is not clearly spelled out in the readings, but references suggest some connection.

In 1944, a young Pennsylvania teen-ager was told:

> Before that we find the entity was in the English land in the early settlings of the children of Israel who were foregathered with the daughters of Hezekiah in what is now Somerland, Somerhill, or Somerset. There the entity

saw group organizations for the preservation
of tenets and truths of the living God, just as
those admonitions would be for the entity in
the present as it begins that social service with
children.

Preserve the law of the Lord. For it is
perfect and it converteth the soul. Not, then,
by might or power but by His word, saith the
Lord of hosts.

In the experience the entity gained, for it
helped in establishing aids to the children of
the period in making better homes, in making
better relationships in the abilities to care for
selves, and as vocational activities . . .

The name then was Ruth. (5384-1)

Altars as well as homes were established:

. . . the entity was in the Holy Land when
there were those breakings up in the periods
when the land was being sacked by the Chaldeans and Persians.

The entity was among those groups who
escaped in the ships that settled in portions
of the English land near what is now Salisbury, and there builded those altars that were
to represent the dedications of individuals to
a service of a living God.

Thus the entity aided in giving the records and teachings that may help others in
the present, in giving to others that helping
hand—who may be as a record keeper.

The name then was Mayra. (3645-1)

A 1938 reading for a missionary writer tells that
not only the religious laws were preserved, but also the
economic laws. Dan, the tribe with a seafaring background, and Judah, the royal tribe, combined efforts:

. . . when there was the breaking up of what has been in our memories or histories given as the taking of the ten tribes, or their dispersing.

The entity then was among those who came into the land now known as the English, and was of those peoples who were the children of one faithful in many ways—being a portion of those descended from the children of Dan and those who had been with Caleb in Bethlehem.

Then the entity was of both those tribes, but entered into the activities in the land for the preservation not only of those manners of worship, those manners of preserving lives, but of the economic laws that had been a part of the experience of those peoples who were the fathers of the entity then—in the name Zedekiah.

In the experience the entity gained, but in the latter portion lost. For the signs, the symbols came to be rather as the purposes than that for which they were brought into being.

Thus the entity failed in that portion. But the entity had a helpful, developing experience in all the manners of health, of sanitation, of diets. (1598-1)

A Minnesota housewife had been one of Hezekiah's grandchildren who went to England. In time the center was absorbed, but it left its stamp upon the nation:

Before that the entity was in the English land during those periods when there was the breaking up of the tribes of Israel.

The entity was a granddaughter of Hezekiah the king, and among those who set sail to escape when the activities brought the rest of the people into servitude in the Persian land.

Then the entity was among those who landed and set up the seat of customs as indicated in the altars built near what is now Salisbury, England. These were the early traditions carried into those activities.

The name then was Elemeshia. The entity gained in the ability as a leader, in the ability to influence others, the ability to control the activities of individuals in such a way as to make for the forming of moral habits and ideas in their material experiences. (3590 –1)

Apparently the migrations stretched over a long period of time, like an underground railway.

Another member of the royal family is found in a 1940 reading:

Before that the entity was in the land now known as the English land, during the very early developments there of a people who were a part of the tribes that had been dispersed with Hezekiah's being carried into captivity in the Chaldean land.

The entity was the younger of the queen's household that came into the England land—the name Ariel. In the experience the entity aided its companions, those of its own household, of its own families or tribes—as they were known in those periods—to establish homes, places of refuge, places for the protection of individuals as well as groups, when hardships or turmoils would arise in their experience.

In the present we find the desires, innate

and manifested, and the channels or outlets through which the greater awareness and consciousness of the abilities to aid may come— in advice with, and in counseling with, others. (2109–2)

The re-establishment of the altars for worship was an important consideration.

The entity was with those people who sought refuge in what is now the English land, and in and about what is now Somerset. The entity was with the groups who had come from even the temple watch in Jerusalem, who established the outer courts or the temple for individual service and activity, as well as the altars which have long since been torn away and yet there are evidences of these having been set up in a form of a court and an inner court for the admonitions and the directions and encouragements to peoples who would learn the Lord.
The name then was Puella. (5276–1)

Altars are again mentioned in this reading from 1944. A South Dakota woman was told:

... the entity was in the English land during those periods when there were the activities from the daughter of Zedekiah, the king, whose activities were cut short and then prolonged by Nebuchadnezzar. There was the founding of those activities in the English land in and about those places where the stones were set up as the altars. These were to represent the tabernacle. These were enlarged upon and these were those experiences of the entity, and thus all forms of mysticism, all forms of occult science, occult influences were a portion of the activity; as the holy of holies, the ephod, Urim and Thummin; all of these were parts of the entity's experience.

The entity then was in the present sex, in the name Judith. The entity guided the interpreting of the worship in the forms which set up discarding blood sacrifice for those as of fruits, yet blood by those that were of another form of same in its activities. Thus relationships which were and are a part of man's experience became abhorrent to the entity in its present period of development. (5259–1)

With the dispersion and the wandering, the Israelites were given new opportunities to establish the seeds and fruits of a universal consciousness. A Jewish man was told:

Before that the entity was in the English land during those periods when there were those journeyings into that land from the Holy Land, when the children of Hezekiah prompted many of those even in authority to leave the Holy Land because of Nebuchadnezzar's activities.

The entity was young in years when it came into the coasts of England where altars were set up to tie up the meanings of "The Lord thy God is one." The building up of this thought makes no bonds, no slaves among any peoples.

The name then was Jeheuh. The entity gained greatly.

Hence the abilities to meet with its fellow man, to control through its personality; that is, being what it is truly and not just to be seen of men but to be seen of its Maker. (3581–1)

The female members of the royal family were actively engaged in the work of resettlement. "The daughters of Hezekiah" are mentioned throughout, probably as a guild. The following describes a daughter of Zedekiah:

> The entity was of the daughters of Zedekiah, and among those who—through the activities of some of the children of Benjamin, Judah and Dan—came to the Isles, and began the establishing of an understanding that the mysteries of the ages that had been handed down to the priests—in the judgment of the records given by the prophets and sages of old —could or might be established in such a form, such a manner as to ever present—to the peoples who looked upon same—a reminder of the promises of Divinity to the children of men—even in their weakness!
>
> Then the entity was in the name Zeurah, and a prophetess—yea, as one given in the understanding of the influences of the seasons, of the years, of the signs as set in what ye call the zodiac, in what ye call the various phases of man's experience.
>
> Hence the entity gained, yet set—as it were—a temptation in the way of others; in that the SYMBOL became to mean more than that for which it had stood!
>
> Man is three-dimensional in his aspects and study of what he finds within and without, and as to its source and its end—yet of the moment and not the whole. For know as of old: "Know, O ye people, the Lord thy God is one!" (1580–1)

One male of the Davidic dynasty also survived. Apparently he escaped the punishment meted to Zedekiah's heirs. He went to England, worked with his hands, and developed spiritually. In 1939, a young Jewish boy was told:

> Before this we find ye—as the grandson of Zedekiah—made for those activities in the land now known as the English, where—with those of thy peoples—ye set up the attempted activity in that land.
>
> There ye went, not a priest but rather as a teacher, a workman with thy hands; as a leader, as a director—in the name then Zeruben.
>
> In the experience ye gained, for ye established freedom of individual activity, yet united in one accord for the common good of all in the material relationships.
>
> The weaknesses of forcing the purposes, the issues, became manifest during the experience; yet these GREW by the tempering of self FOR the greater purposes to be those lessons that ye may apply in this present experience. (1856–1)

IRELAND

The Irish have a long-standing tradition that Jeremiah, the prophet, came with the remnant of the royal tribe of David and established a settlement in Ireland.

This reading speaks of an Irish colony. In 1939, an incarnation as Zedekiah's granddaughter was described for a six-year-old girl:

> Before that we find the entity was in the land now known as the Promised Land, during those periods when there was the breaking up of the land under the king who was carried away captive into the Persian land.
>
> There we find the entity was a granddaughter of that king, Zedekiah, in the name

Zelka; among those peoples who escaped from the activities under Nebuchadnezzar's forces and took ship for that now known as Ireland.

There we find the entity was among those who set up or established a part of a settlement in that land. Hence then of a hardy people, those accustomed to things that would have to do with the out-of-doors . . .

In the experiences then we find the entity developed through those activities, bringing about the greater longings for places and activities where there might be the better mental and spiritual interpretations of those things that had been handed down to its peoples as customs, as things that happened in the varied ways and manners as legends of its peoples, legends of its leaders, its kings, and those who went not to stand before— those of the powers of the south and the east and the north and the west. All of these are latent within the experience of the entity in the present sojourn. (2005–1)

ON THE ALTARS OF THE WORLD

Wherever the scattered people went—America, Mexico, England, or Babylon—they established altars. Although this extract describes altars in Yucatan, it is the premise behind the activities in all the newly settled lands. The work has always been to lead souls back to the universal consciousness.

The altars upon which there were the cleansings of the bodies of individuals (not human sacrifice . . .), these were later the altars upon which individual activities—that would today be termed hate, malice, selfishness, self-indulgence—were cleansed from the body through the ceremony, through the rise of initiates from the sources of light, that came from the stones upon which the angels of light during the periods gave their expression to the peoples. (5750–1)

8

Judah in Babylon

"When ye forsake my ways ye shall be
scattered, ye shall be without those things that
would bring ye into the knowledge—until
that time is fulfilled." (3976–13)

The Israelites were called to establish the kingdom of
God on earth, but where the kingdom was to be built,
and how, was frequently misunderstood. Only a few,
like David, knew it had to start from within.

As time passed, more and more of Israel's energy,
thought and emotion was devoted to the material aspects and preservation of the kingdom, and less and
less to its original spiritual intent and purpose. As the
people became more enmeshed and involved with the
outward forms, they lost sight of the inner principles
through which the kingdom had come.

As captive slaves, Judah finally found the time to
do that which it had failed while free—to find God.

The Cayce material tells us that wherever we
are, in whatever condition we find ourselves, is the
place we must begin to search for God. Judah had a
multitude of opportunities in a variety of changing
circumstances to search for and know God. As a free
nation and in days of plenty, they gradually forgot and
forsook those creative and spiritual principles which

had formed and shaped the nation under Joshua, the Judges, and David. By forgetting God, they forgot about their souls and lost sight of the only power that could perpetuate the nation.

Although occasionally they were called back to the light by prophets and kings to enjoy renewed strength, vitality, and prosperity, they ultimately degenerated all the resources which had been given them. They were called to the light, only to drift back into the darkness. Over and over again the nation repeated this cycle, sliding ever closer to the final tragedy and national trauma when the "day of reckoning" arrived. They had misused and abused everything that had been entrusted to them, now everything was taken away—everything except God.

The captivity was caused by the same disregard that had brought on the deluge.

> . . . the deluge was not a myth . . . but a period when man had so belittled himself with the cares of the world, with the deceitfulness of his own knowledge and power, as to require that there be a return to his dependence wholly—physically and mentally—upon the Creative Forces. (3653-1)

A Jewish businessman was told in his reading that he had been among "the sons of Moses," a direct descendant, and that the spiritual lesson of the captivity was not lost on him.

> The entity gained through this experience, for those waitings, those openings of the hearts of the peoples in an alien or foreign land brought many lessons to the entity, that service to man is the highest service that may be rendered to the God. This the entity has lost in, somewhat, in the present, yet is there

that bond ever present that self must be in touch *with* that upon which one may lean, not only in dire circumstances, but in joys, in pleasures, in hardships, in trials . . . (426–2)

In captivity the Jews were forced into introspection and re-evaluation. They had time to question their direction and, aided by great prophets like Daniel, Jeremiah, and Ezekiel, awaken with humility and obedience to the Spirit and to their service to man.

Although the seventy years of captivity was a time in which the traditions and religious experiences of the past became "hearsay" (2305–2), and much was neglected by the teachers and interpreters of the law (2444–1), and a great deal of drunkenness or dissipation prevailed among the Jews who were favored with high positions in the court (1096–2), there was also that important "remnant," that immeasurably valuable handful, who kept clear of all these influences and searched for God.

It was the people who entertained the spirit of God within who had the most influence on their captors. Deep calls to deep, the psalmist said, and spirit to spirit. Both the Chaldeans and the Jews were sons of God. As the Jews reawakened to the universal spirit of the Father-God in them, it drew out a response from the same spirit within the Chaldean, and later the Persian, so that all could work together for the fulfillment of God's will—that not one soul should perish. Thus Jeremiah counseled the captive Jews in Babylon not to resist the bondage, but to "seek the peace of the city" where they had been taken and "to pray for it." (Jeremiah 29:7) Only by finding God in the place where they found themselves could they ever become at-one with His spirit and agents of His will.

If service to man is the highest service to God (426–2), and the greater service to man is "awakening an individual to the consciousness of that presence which may abide within" (2787–1), as slaves the Jews were in a unique position to serve. Through their long and highly developed relationship with the creative forces, with the added impetus given through David and Solomon, the nation had much to give in the fields of wisdom, art, and science.

Some vivid accounts of the *spiritual* service are found in the Book of Daniel. Several life readings of this period give additional insights into the ability of the "slaves" to lift the consciousness of their captors.

AN ACCOUNT OF SLAVERY

Nebuchadnezzar recognized the superiority of the Jews, and ordered the flower of the population to grace his court.

> *And the king spoke of Ashpaz the chief of his eunuchs, that he should bring some of the children of Israel, of the royal families and the nobility, youths without blemish, handsome and skilful in all wisdom, endowed with knowledge, understanding learning, and competent to serve in the king's palace, and to teach them the letters and language of the Chaldeans. (Daniel 1:4)*

The following reading amplifies this text as it describes the experience of a Jewish maiden in the courts of Babylon:

> Before that we find the entity was in the land when the children of promise were among those who were carried away captive.
>
> There we find the entity was among those of the then Chaldean or Persian land, during

those periods when there were the activities under Nebuchadnezzar; and there we find the entity was among those whom the lords of Nebuchadnezzar's army had besieged.

Thus we find the entity coming into those activities in which persecutions were not exactly the nature, because the entity became a slave, for the slaves in that experience were those who were learned in the arts or in what ye call science, or in what ye call beautiful speech or poetry or art, or ALL of those things. For that was thought by those to be rather only the work of those who had the time or the period to devote to such study.

Again, then, we find the entity gave expression in song, in music upon the harp—not in the shape of the harp known today, but the harp of the period, that was much in the shape of a butterfly wing.

But the longings for the hills of its native land, the songs for those periods of sacrifice, the songs for those periods of rejoicing—all brought to the land that which eventually—through its evolution in the hearts and minds of those peoples—brought redemption FOR the entity's people, that came again in the much later periods to its own land again. The entity did not see the land—it in the material plane knew little of that which brought such about, yet deep and innate within self is felt, from the activities, the JOY of being good—not only because of its innate abilities but the harmony as created within the very BEING itself, and the great abilities that may arise in the experience of those who PRACTICE such in their daily life.

The name then was Estha—of the peoples led away by the first of the armies of Nebuchadnezzar FROM the regions about Jerusalem—and of the daughters of Rechab. (1934-1)

As can be imagined, not all slaves enjoyed their position. The following reading pictures a young Jewish beauty forced into "abhorrent" activities by her captors.

> Before that we find the entity was in the land now called the Persian, or a portion of India or Mesopotamia and those portions of the lands to which the chosen peoples were taken as captives—or in bondage.
>
> Hence the entity was of those that were close in the household of Zedekiah, the king carried into Babylon.
>
> Because of the beauty, because of the abilities of the entity, it found favor among the leaders of the soldiery and thus was protected; but became—by force, not by choice —as a pawn among those leaders. Thus it was forced into activities that were abhorrent to the individual's self in the experience.
>
> Yet from the MENTAL forces the entity gained.
>
> As to the activities from that sojourn, we find in the present the love of ease; the abilities to find grace or favor—many of these come from those experiences; as does the love of soft things, the delicate things close to the body—and yet the knowledge of [what] all these imply is as an innate force in the experience.
>
> The name then was Shasdacha. (1522-1)

The readings make it clear that every incarnation is influenced and conditioned by the lives which preceded it. It is the Biblical law of "what ye sow, so shall ye reap." Although the two entities above were in the collective karma of their nation, both knowing slavery, their individual experiences were diverse and unique, the result of activities begun in former lives.

In the preceding life, both entities had incarnated in Egypt during the same period; [1934] gained spiritually as an instructor in "artistic manners and forms" for use as home decorations and temple services. The good vibrations set up in that life influenced her opportunities and experience as a slave in Babylon.

In Egypt [1522] ministered to the sick and afflicted in hospital service, but as she rose to position and authority, turned to self-indulgence and "brought for itself that of condemnation." The bad vibrations of her Egyptian life were encountered karmicly through those "abhorrent" activities inflicted by the self-indulgence of her Babylonian captors.

Although our local, national, or world communities may be building karmic conditions which will be met on an inevitable "day of reckoning" our experiences within the pattern need not be traumatic nor bitter. When Jesus spoke of the great tribulation of the "latter days" he urged his disciples to pray and avoid the things of the world which burden the spirit in order to be "worthy to escape" from those things which were bound to happen. (Luke 21:34–36) These two readings, in the great cycle of the last days of the Jewish monarchy, show the universal and timeless validity of doing good.

DANIEL

Among the most memorable events during the captivity are found in the Book of Daniel and revolve around the experiences and visions of the prophet for whom the book is named.

Reading 3976–15 contains a clear indication that Jacob and John the Beloved were incarnations of the same soul. The reading states that this entity is "one beloved of all men in all places where the universality of God in the earth has been proclaimed . . ." No figure in the Old Testament is more beloved than Daniel. Comparisons between the Book of Daniel and the Revelation reveal a similarity which strongly suggests Daniel as another incarnation of John. (See the visions of the beasts, prophecies of the latter days, and compare Daniel 8:15–19 with Revelation 1:17; 22:8.) Jacob, Daniel, and John—the dreams and visions of these three beloved figures have guided, shaped, and opened man's consciousness to the glories of God.

In the first chapter of Daniel, the prophet takes a stand.

> *But Daniel resolved that he would not defile himself with the king's rich food, or with the wine which he drank. (Daniel 1:8)*

This reading tells why.

> As has been given of old, when the children of Israel stood with the sons of the heathen, and all ate from the king's table, that which was taken that only exercised the imagination of the body in physical desires— as strong drink, strong meats, condiments that magnify desires with the body—this builded, as Daniel well understood, not for God's service . . . he chose, rather, that the everyday, the common things would be given, so that the bodies, the minds might be a more perfect channel for the manifestations of God; for the forces of the Creator are in every force that is made manifest in the earth. (341–31)

Daniel and Nebuchadnezzar

How can anyone interpret a dream when its contents are not known? This was the task Nebuchadnezzar put to his astrologers, magicians, and sorcerers after his spirit became troubled by a dream. (Daniel 2) He refused to divulge the dream, and promised riches and reward to the one who could tell him the dream and its meaning, and death to all if an interpretation was not forthcoming.

This was a difficult task, but not an impossible one. According to Edgar Cayce, the Chaldeans were the first people to give psychic readings. (3744–1) They began about 4000 B.C., the reading asserts, and were given as a means to assist the flow of the life-giving forces of soul and spirit to and through the physical body—a description which applies equally as well to the Edgar Cayce readings!

Apparently the psychic arts were lost to the Chaldeans by Nebuchadnezzar's time, approximately a thousand years later, for there was no one among his wise men who possessed the psychic sensitivities to meet the unusual situation created by Nebuchadnezzar.

Edgar Cayce was often asked to interpret forgotten dreams. Instances of this are found frequently in the 900 series, and in other readings as well. Other times, when dreams were written out and submitted for interpretation, Cayce elaborated upon the forgotten elements of the dream which had not been recorded. The reading would often stimulate instant recall by the dreamer who then was able to confirm the accuracy of the interpretation.

In a reading devoted to the subject of "psychic phenomena," Cayce discussed his own ability to gather information while in the psychic state:

> In this [trance] state the conscious mind becomes subjugated to the subconscious, superconscious, or soul-mind; and may and does communicate with like minds, and the subconscious or soul force becomes universal. From any subconscious mind informa-

tion may be obtained, either from this plane or from the impressions as left by the individuals that have gone on before. (3744–2)

Speaking of the trance state again, in another reading we find:

. . . in this body [Cayce] lying here, we find all life in suspension; only portions of the higher vibrations in accord with those vibrations that communicate with the universal forces. (900–10)

Apparently Edgar Cayce was able to achieve the same attunement with the universal as Daniel.

The decree that all the wise men of Babylon would be slain included Daniel and his companions. Daniel besought the king for an appointment, then he returned to his house and, with his friends, prayed that God would reveal the dream and its meaning.

That night while Daniel's conscious mind and physical body were in that state of "suspension" called sleep (or deep meditation) his subconscious and superconscious minds were in attune with the universal forces, and he received the vision. Apparently he attuned his mind to the subconscious mind of Nebuchadnezzar and the impressions his dream had created upon it.

Daniel went to Nebuchadnezzar and recounted his dream and its meaning. Daniel's accuracy is confirmed through Nebuchadnezzar's reaction:

Then King Nebuchadnezzar fell upon his face, and did homage to Daniel, and commanded that an offering and incense be offered up to him. The king said to Daniel, "Truly, your God is God of gods and Lord of kings, and a revealer of mysteries, for you have been able to reveal this mystery." Then the king gave Daniel high honors and

*many great gifts and made him ruler over the
whole province of Babylon and chief prefect over
all the wise men of Babylon. (Daniel 2:46)*

THE FIERY FURNACE

Daniel was either an able teacher or among a
group in an advanced state of consciousness. When
Nebuchadnezzar built an enormous statue of solid gold
and ordered all the officials of his kingdom to bow
down and worship it, Shadrach, Meshach, and Abednego refused. The king was enraged and threatened the
men with death in a fiery furnace.

The men were unshaken, and answered:

*"O Nebuchadnezzar, we have no need to an-
swer you in this matter. If it be so, our God whom
we serve is able to deliver us from the burning
fiery furnace; and he will deliver us out of your
hand, O king. But if not, be it known to you, O
king, that we will not serve your gods or worship
the golden image which you have set up." (Daniel
3:16)*

The men were cast into the furnace, and were not
consumed. They walked about singing and praying
with a fourth person whom Nebuchadnezzar discerned
through the flames. (Daniel 3:25)

Apparently it was a total absorption with the
God-consciousness which worked the miracle of deliverance, as the following reading will indicate.

A dream reading was requested by a young Jewish stockbroker with pronounced psychic ability. The
reading was the eighty-eighth in his series. In the pre-
amble, Cayce said of the dreamer:

In the dreams as are seen as presented to
this entity, more and more come those visions
of that in which and through which the entity

139

may gain for self that insight into that full consciousness of the strength that lies from within, when once attuned to that consciousness that brings those lessons, those experiences, to the body-conscious mind through the subconscious forces of the entity, and the entity may gain in mental, physical, and financial manners from same. Ready for dream. (137–88)

A dramatic dream with an obvious parallel to the fiery furnace was submitted.

Evening of September 30, or morning of October 1, 1929. A direct comparison between the essence or heat energy in fire and the essence or human energy of Man. Both seemed one and the same substance or force. I, or someone, jumped into the fire to prove this oneness. Someone else thought that I or the person who jumped in the fire to indicate that the force of my inner self and the outer world are one and the same force or God, was crazy. The person in the fire seemed to have a peculiar expression, but felt no pain. (137–88)

The answer gives an insight into men of the fiery furnace.

The entity sees, visions, here is an experience that is as one of the lessons as proof to the entity of the oneness of all force, energy, or what not, varied in its various aspects, and the entity in studying same, and the effect upon the individual, gains an insight into the lessons as would be studied by the entity—for, as is seen, all energy set in motion becomes an applied force in its application, and, as is seen, when one universal law, whether of human energy or of that in an *element,* as is created by the energy meeting those laws through the combustibility, as is called fire, then we see how that only at a different angle does each present itself to the consciousness of man, and man making self, then, in the at-onement with the forces, is able to overcome or demonstrate the whole oneness, yet man, conscious of the other variations *in* the one force, feels the burning pain, and not the at-oneness. (137–88)

The miracle of the fiery furnace had an indirect effect as a spiritual service. Like Daniel's revelation, it brought Nebuchadnezzar to the point of conversion.

> Then Nebuchadnezzar came near to the door of the burning fiery furnace and said, "Shadrach, Meshach, and Abednego, servants of the Most High God, come forth, and come here." Then Shadrach, Meshach, and Abednego came out from the fire. And the satraps, the prefects, the governors, and the king's counselors gathered and saw that the fire had not had any power over the bodies of those men; the hair of their heads was not singed, their mantles were not harmed, and no smell of fire had come upon them.
> Nebuchadnezzar said, "Blessed be the God of Shadrach, Meshach, and Abednego, who has sent his angel and delivered his servants, who trusted in him, and set at nought the king's command, and yielded up their bodies rather than serve and worship any god except their own God. Therefore I make a decree: . . . for there is no other god who is able to deliver in this way."

Then the king promoted Shadrach, Meshach, and Abednego in the province of Babylon. (Daniel 3:26–30)

Daniel in the lion's den (Daniel 6) may be explained by the same principle. Daniel's awareness of God's presence was so all-pervasive that he saw the lion as a creation of God rather than the wild, fearful creature men have been conditioned to seeing. Thus he and the lion were at-one with the same spirit and no harm came to either.

NEBUCHADNEZZAR'S MADNESS AND THE TREE OF LIFE

The fourth chapter of Daniel consists of a letter which Nebuchadnezzar had circulated throughout his kingdom. It is the account of his madness which possessed him for seven years, rendering him as a "beast of the field" and the dream which had previewed this condition and the interpretation which Daniel had accurately ascribed to it.

Nebuchadnezzar had several dramatic examples shown him of the power of God manifesting through man. He recognized the spirit and had awakened to it himself by showing mercy and forgiveness, yet he could not turn away from the self-indulgent pleasures of his court life, nor from the ego-centered imaginations of his own mind. The same conflict had driven Saul to madness and led to the death of pharaoh who had hardened his heart after witnessing the increasing manifestations of Moses' spiritual power.

The Tree of Life in Genesis 2 is a symbol of man's soul in true attunement with God. In the Revelation, the Tree of Life symbolizes the soul, or entity, whose purposes are rooted in the spirit of the Christ. (281-37)

In Nebuchadnezzar's dream, he saw a great tree growing in the midst of the earth.

142

"The tree grew and became strong, and its top reached to heaven, and it was visible to the end of the whole earth. Its leaves were fair and its fruit abundant, and in it was food for all. The beasts of the field found shade under it, and the birds of the air dwelt in its branches, and all flesh was fed from it." (Daniel 4:11–12)

An angel intrudes in the dream and hews the tree down, and proclaims:

"Let his mind be changed from a man's and let a beast's mind be given to him and let seven times pass over him." (Daniel 4:16)

The angel then declares the purpose for this is to teach men that the Most High rules the kingdoms of men and gives it to whomever He wills.

Daniel was to the point in his interpretation of the Tree.

"It is you, O king, who have grown and become strong." (Daniel 4:22)

The downfall portended in the dream came from separation and Nebuchadnezzar's true lack of understanding as to the real source of his power and ability. His ego, his passions and desires, brought on his downfall and his madness. After seven years, he experienced a complete change in consciousness and a new understanding. He was a little bit closer to being the true "tree of life" which never falls.

At the end of the days I, Nebuchadnessar, lifted my eyes to heaven, and my reason returned to me, and I blessed the Most High and praised and honored him who lives forever; for his dominion is an everlasting dominion, and his kingdom endures from generation to generation . . .

*At the same time my reason returned to me;
and for the glory of my kingdom, my majesty, and
splendor returned to me. My counselors and my
lords sought me, and I was established in my
kingdom, and still more greatness was added to
me. How I, Nebuchadnezzar, praise and extol
and honor the king of heaven; for all his works
are right and his ways are just; and those who
walk in pride he is able to abase." (Daniel
4:34–37)*

The counsel in this reading applies equally to
Nebuchadnezzar's experience.

So will He, that is the Maker of Heaven and
earth, He that is the uprising and the down-
sitting of all mankind, bring to thy life and
thy experience that necessary for thy greatest
development—and peace and harmony within self will be the result, if thy purposes,
thy desires, thy labors are spent in the activity for others, rather than attempting to
justify ideas of any moral, physical, or mental relationships.
Know that truth and honor need no justi-
fication; rather the glorifying of same only is
righteousness in the sight of thy Maker.
(2061–1)

This queen of Nebuchadnezzar's learned a lesson
by observation.

Before that the entity was in the Persian
land, during those periods when peoples were
brought in as chattels, or as servants, from
other lands.
For, the entity then was one of the royal
family, being the wife of the king during
that experience; knowing then much of the

madness of Nebuchadnezzar, as well as of the sojourns of the peoples under bondage.

Those were periods that will be expressive in the present experiences of the entity; that those things of material security, that are of the worldly nature, are the less secure than friends and spiritual peace—spiritual peace from knowing that there is that activity in the relationships to individuals, no matter what their position in life may be—that ye should do to them as ye would desire to be done to thee if circumstances were altered, or reversed.

Those lessons learned then by the entity, even from those who were servants to the entity, may be those that may keep the balance in the experiences through this present sojourn . . .

The name then was Sczeldhardi. In the experience the entity suffered mentally, the entity was exalted materially, the entity sought gratification of self's own indulgences; and yet in the later portion the entity gained through trouble, turmoil, and the deposing of the powers—with the madness of the companion. (2468–1)

CAPTIVES AND THEIR MASTERS

The great service of spiritual awakening was performed in less dramatic ways than the events recorded in Daniel. The Jewish slaves as they searched for and awakened to the Spirit had a subtle but lasting effect upon their Chaldean captors, as several readings testify. The presence of the spirit was over all. The following describe the various awakenings and manifestations of the spirit in the lives of those who lived in Babylon through this period.

Jewish slaves played a role in the spiritual awakening of this Chaldean. Although in authority, this entity felt uneasiness in his soul as he looked upon the conquered peoples:

> Before that the entity was in the Chaldean land, during those periods when there were peoples gathering there from other lands.
>
> The entity then was one close in authority to those who ruled in the land, during the period of Nebuchadnezzar and those closely following same.
>
> Hence we find that the entity enjoyed the blessings, or curses (dependent upon their use), which the natural sources and resources had to offer. Yet the entity was not wholly pleased with the happenings, because of the social environs as well as the lack of harmony —in those periods—in the mental and spiritual development of the peoples.
>
> The entity then heard many mournings of a people, and of many peoples of varied lands—and combined what may be called the true oriental music (or the mourns) with the joys of those who put their trust wholly in, and looked for, redeeming force and power.
>
> Then the name was Helzonput—the entity gained, lost, and gained; gained in the very desire to keep the helpful influences in the minds of those with whom the entity came in contact, so as to bring joy and harmony; lost in the turning of these influences for self's own gain, and in the exerting of same for self's own indulgences.
>
> But from that sojourn we find in the present that great abilities arise from deep within, to wield a power of might, as well as the still small voice of love and hope. (2132–1)

A Jewish housewife was told that as a young captive she kept her faith:

> . . . when the entity's peoples were being carried away into captivity by the Persians, or by Nebuchadnezzar and his horde and hosts.
>
> The entity was among the younger people who were thus carried away, yet its sincerity of purpose in keeping its tenets as to its relationships to Creative Forces, or those things that had been taught by those of its own household, brought hardships—but harmony—by the very influence of such in the experience, though in a strange land.
>
> The name then was Elkan. (2061-1)

This reading speaks of Chaldean cruelty and a lesson to be learned:

> The entity was among the leaders of Nebuchadnezzar's forces, in the name then Xerteiun.
>
> In the experience the entity made for that which finds expression in the present; as to its politics, its home, its business being as separate things in the life.
>
> But know the truth of that which was taught by those priests whom ye heard of old, and those upon whom you made many stripes for the announcing of their faith (or had it done) that "The Lord thy God is ONE!" Know that their law is true. While life and death are the opposites, they are constant companions one with another. Only the destructive forces know death as lord. Only spiritual or creative forces know life AS the Lord. Know YE the Lord! (1432-1)

The spiritual influence from the Jewish slaves formed deep-seated spiritual insights for this Babylonian leader—with results which helped later to free the captive people. In 1940 an Austrian housewife was told:

> Before that the entity was in the Chaldean land, during those periods when a people became as servants, as chattel of that land OVER which, THROUGH which, the entity had influence and power.
>
> For the entity was of the household of one Beltzadader, a leader of one of Nebuchadnezzar's armed groups.
>
> There the entity gained greatly in its abilities to apply some of those tenets gathered from those who became servants to the entity through a portion of that experience.
>
> And the entity applied same in its relationships or dealings with others—not as to what might be termed its court or social life, other than in a general manner; yet the purposes, the intents, the activities of the entity then—as Shalazur—were those tenets, those principles that years later made for the creating of that which FREED a peoples, under those determinations and activities of Xerxes; also at those periods of the return of that people who had taught much to the entity, through those tenets and principles of the young, who had been instructed in that law which is universal—"As ye would that men should do to you, do ye even so to them."
>
> It is simple in words, yet so deep in its meaning, so far-reaching in its application in every phase of human experience! For it is the opposite of greed, avarice, hate, and that which makes people afraid. (2170-1)

This princess was added in her natural spiritual development by her Jewish slaves.

> Before that the entity was in the Chaldean land, during those periods when there were other lands brought under submission—politically.
>
> The entity then was a princess in that land. Yet, coming under the care of some of those that were as but slaves, the entity gained by that association.
>
> Abilities as a danseuse, abilities as an artist, abilities as a musician, arise from the entity's application of the tenets gained in the youth, in the meeting of the problems in the court during those periods of activity—even in the court of Nebuchadnezzar, the king in Babylonia. Though the entity was of the Babylonians, it was not as those of the legends; of Babylon but not a Babylonian. For, the entity applied its abilities not to excite or to satisfy the selfish appetites, but rather was known for its beauty, its grace, its dependability in developing body and mind to those of the beauties rather than the low, the mean things as may arise from gratifying appetites.
>
> The name then was Schardezrah. And this was one of the great material experiences of the body-entity . . . For there were the purposes, the desires for the manifesting of beauty and grace among those with whom the entity constantly came in contact through that sojourn.
>
> It is well to use those promptings in this present experience. (2559–1)

Although one of Zedekiah's daughters (1580) and two grandchildren (1856, 2005) escaped to England, at least one daughter went to Babylon and worked for the release of her people. A young Virginia housewife was told:

> The entity then was among the princesses of the Jewish peoples, or of the daughters of Zedekiah, who was carried into the Babylonian land; becoming associated with those who were in authority during those periods when there was the re-establishing of that people, in the Persian and Chaldean land . . .
>
> Then the entity was in the name Esmara, and the entity aided in establishing among its own peoples that desire which later found expression before those in authority for the return of the peoples to the worship and the rebuilding in the Holy City.
>
> In the experience, then, the entity gained the greater concept as to how to be, and not to be, the more helpful in all environs, in whatever might be the activities or the associations. (1857–2)

9

Liberation

BELSCHAZZAR AND THE FALL OF BABYLON

The Babylonian empire scarcely outlived its founder, Nebuchadnezzar. The empire lasted seventy years, exactly coincident with the seventy years of captivity, over which Nebuchadnezzar reigned forty-five. Approximately twenty-five years after his death, the mighty empire collapsed under Belschazzar.

Shortly after Daniel interpreted "the handwriting on the wall" (Daniel 5), Babylon was taken by Cyrus the Great and supremacy passed to Persia.

The dissipation among the ruling class led to decay and weakness, and for Belschazzar created karmic knots which have yet to be untied.

A reading for a young musician began with an analysis:

> Many peoples are doubted by the entity. Many are weighed in the balance of mental ability by the entity and found wanting. Truly might it be said of the entity, as is seen in one of the experiences, that "MENE MENE TEKEL UPHARSIN" to the entity ever stands before the entity; for to this en-

tity the handwriting was *real*—being the king in power and ruler at that period. (4609–1)

The experience as Belschazzar was described:

... we find the entity that ruler, that king in power, when the handwriting was given that those would be measured in the balance and those found wanting would be called to reckoning. The entity then lost through that experience, and in those forces that deal with the physical application or physical *result* of application of abilities we find the entity meriting many of those hardships through which the present experience brings to the entity; yet with all that, the love of harmony, that of the ability to listen ever for that warning, brings much to the entity, and— applied in the present sphere—may bring the development of the entity far along the way of gaining the more perfect understanding... (4609–1)

DREAMS AND THE FALL OF BABYLON

Unusual events surround the fall of Babylon. The handwriting on the wall was part of a precognitive prologue. Nebuchadnezzar's dream of the tree with the gold and silver bands around the trunk, also interpreted by Daniel, was another preview. (Daniel 2) Until the seventeenth century, Babylon was unsurpassed for its beauty, art, science, and power. Thus it was the most precious and imaged as "gold" in Nebuchadnezzar's dream. The Persian regime which followed this was strong and glorious, but fell short of Babylon's glory. Thus it was represented as "silver," a precious metal but inferior to gold.

The conquerer of Babylon, Cyrus, was also a soul of destiny, and unusual dreams surround his birth.

When Cyrus' mother was still a young girl and a virgin, her father had a dream in which he saw a stream of water flowing from his daughter that flooded the whole Asian continent. During her term of pregnancy, Astyages had another vision. In the second he saw a vine growing from his daughter's womb that overshadowed Asia. The Magi interpreted both as portends of the destiny of his daughter's child—Cyrus the Great.

In 559 B.C. Cyrus began a revolt against the Median empire. Through a series of brilliant campaigns, he was able to unite many disaffected elements among the Medes; and in 540 he marched against Babylon.

The conquest of Babylon itself was unprecedented in the military annals of the orient. The city was taken without bloodshed, struggle, or the loss of life.

A clay cylinder of Cyrus' describes what took place:

> As I entered Babylon in peace, and established my royal residence in the palace amid jubilation and rejoicing, Marduk,* the great lord, warmed the hearts of the Babylonians toward me, while I for my part devoted myself daily to do him reverence. My troops wandered peacefully widespread throughout Babylon. In all Sumer and Akkad I let no man be afraid. I concerned myself with the internal affairs of Babylon and all its cities. The dwellers in Babylon . . . I freed from the yoke that ill became them. I repaired their houses, I healed their afflictions . . . I am Cyrus, king of all, the great king of the four corners of the earth.

With this triumph, Cyrus became master over western Asia, establishing an empire that stretched from India and Greece to the borders of Egypt.

---

*Marduk was the chief Chaldean god.

In contrast to the brutal patterns of conquest and subjugation by the Assyrian and Babylonian kings, Cyrus' swift and brilliant rise to power was unmarred by atrocities and unusual violence. Whereas the Assyrians and Babylonians deported conquered nationals, Cyrus let them go back home.

The Bible pictures Cyrus as an enlightened king. His achievements reveal a man of broad and universal vision, an admirable and attractive figure among the despots of the ancient oriental world.

The author of many humane policies, Cyrus respected all religions. He honored the gods of Babylon, repaired their temples, and restored the cult statues. He followed a similar policy in Egypt.

In 538 B.C., in the first year of his regime, he fulfilled the vision of Isaiah, who had foreseen Cyrus a century earlier (Isaiah 44:28, 45:1), and the prophecies of Jeremiah, when he authorized the return of the Jews to Palestine and made arrangements for rebuilding the ravaged temple in Jerusalem.

One reading reminds us that the spirit of Christ is eternal and a part of every age:

> Ye have seen His Spirit in the leaders in all realms of activity, whether in the isles of the sea, the wilderness, the mountain, or in the various activities of every race, every color . . . (5749-5)

The Spirit of Christ moves through all men in all nations at all times to bring to completion God's cosmic plan of redemption and salvation. Cyrus, king of Persia, contributed to that plan. By releasing the Jews he was not favoring a nation but giving a blessing to all mankind.

An elderly Virginia housewife, a Christian Scientist, was told of her life as Cyrus' queen. The reading alludes to the universality of purpose in Cyrus—that there might be "the good of all."

Before that the entity was in the Persian or Babylonian land, when there had arisen the desires upon the part of Cyrus that there be given the opportunity for the varied groups over which he had become the power and might, to manifest in their OWN ways and manners; that it might be to the good of all.

The entity then was the queen, Amasmam. In the experience the entity gained greatly by its aid and help to those who were allowed, under the edicts as directed by the king, to return to the Promised Land and there to rebuild the worship which to them had become—then—merely a thing of which they had heard.

Thus the entity was in close association with Zerubbabel and those of his household —Nehemiah, who was a favorite of the entity during his service at the court, and who has been a part of the experiences of this entity in associations through activities in the earth more than in that experience alone.

The entity brought a helpful influence toward the educating of those who were to interpret the law, and to make same accessible.

Thus we find the abilities of the entity in the study of various groups, cults or isms, denominations, political and economic forces as may relate to groups or to states or to nations. And the entity's counsel in such is not to be passed over lightly.

In this experience, then, through its abilities as a speaker, a lecturer, a writer upon such subjects, the entity may bring that measure of service in which there may be AGAIN much given to others in their search for God—even as this was the motive prompting the entity's interest in these activities through that particular sojourn.

Yet also from that sojourn there is the urge for pomp, for having one's own way, for being in authority, and those influences that make for the feelings at times of superiority in so many little material things that are to be curbed in the entity's present experience.

Thus there has been brought many a trial to the physical influences or activities, through the stubbornness—rather has it been self-will, and not intentionally has the entity been dictatorial or stubborn. (2523-1)

This reading supplies an interesting dimension to the Bible story. A young Alabama woman was told she had been Cyrus' daughter. This princess fell in love with Nehemiah, the great Jewish hero of the later period.

Cayce counseled the former princess on the meaning of love as he interpreted her experience:

Before that the entity was in the Persian land in those experiences when there were the preparations for the return of a peoples to build a city to their God.

What, who, where is thy God? Just as ye experienced, as ye saw as the daughter of Cyrus who issued the decree to bring about these changes in the lands. These were disturbing for ye knew not how to apply. Yet they answered to something within thy activities then, in the name Purcelus.

It may be said that the entity gained, for there was the attempt to apply the teachings of those individuals. For, the entity then was very much in love with the cup bearer to the king, Nehemiah. And yet kept separate, kept aloof because of the religious as well as social conditions in the experience.

Remember, true love knows not barriers of any kind that are only of man's creation. For man is the co-creator with the builder and the maker of the universe, and yet creates conditions, positions, thoughts, that often turn and rend his own self. These were builded through the experience because of social positions, but the entity gained. For it learned a lesson of patience, as well as the abilities to sing and to play—if it would— and to dance well.

All of these have their place in the experience, but use them to the glory of God the more often, rather than for the mere satisfaction of the social or body emotions . . .

As the daughter of the king, the most powerful king in the earth at the time, and one called of God to set the house in order for those who felt themselves superior even to the king and yet were subject to him, ye found within thine own self abilities that are still latent. Do not dissipate them, but use them to the glory of God. (3351–1)

This woman was told she not only aided those who encouraged the king, but also knew the rebuilding must start from within.

The entity then was among those peoples that aided in persuading the king who gave helpful advice and counsel to Zerubbabel, encouraging the hearts of Ezra and Nehemiah.

For the entity then was that one or as one who had not neglected the counsel of these who had given, "Keep these laws upon thine heart; bind them upon thine forehead; teach them to thy children that they depart not from the Lord."

Hence the entity was as the mother of those who would remember, bringing to those that were the leaders the encouragement necessary; not only for the trials of the passage but encouraged them in building in their lives and hearts and associations as one to another the remembrance of that which had been given, "Separate yourself if ye would become as those that would know the Lord and His ways!" And as these activities went forward, the entity gave the blessings to those, though not seeing the city nor its rebuilding herself.

Then in the name Esdrus. (1290–1)

BABYLON SYMBOLIZES SELF

If, as the readings suggest, the story "from Abraham to Christ" in a blueprint, or pattern, of mental unfoldment (281–63) and the whole Bible, from Genesis to Revelation, is the complete story or pattern of man in the earth, demonstrating all his potential within for good and for evil, then Babylon, appearing near the end of the completed pattern, holds meaning and significance. Babylon has great importance in the Old Testament, and is a primary symbol in the Revelation of St. John, that last and most enigmatic book of the New Testament which Cayce believed held the key to the meaning of the whole Bible.

Both John and Isaiah prophesied the destruction of Babylon. Although Isaiah's pronouncements were directed toward the historical city, and John's were warnings for the early Christians, both prophecies were directed at the same condition—the selfishness of man.

Babylon represents a condition of consciousness, a state of mind and being. The city symbolizes the ideal of earthly pleasure and excesses of every kind, including misuse of the occult. It is the symbol of man led to a false awareness through the pursuit of selfish desire.

The dirge of Babylon which Isaiah sang for the city (Isaiah 47) can be applied equally well to any world-weary individual.

> *Your knowledge and your wisdom have misled you, and you have said in your heart I am, and there is none else beside me. . . . You are wearied with the multitude of your thoughts. (Isaiah 47:10, 13)*

An interpretation was asked of the Babylon of the Revelation.

Q–12. Does Babylon symbolize self?
A–12. Babylon symbolizes self.
Q–13. Does Revelation 18 give some idea in symbols of the effect of the fall of self—[or] selfishness?
A–13. It does. (281–36)

In an earlier reading, Cayce was asked to interpret the fall of Babylon as described by John in the fourteenth, seventeenth, and eighteenth chapters of the Revelation. Because it is a pattern of *every* soul's experience, the answer is included here.

Babylon represented the individual; those periods through which every soul passes in its delving into the varied mysteries that are the experiences of the carnal-mental, the spiritual-mental forces of the body; and, as viewed from that presented, may come to the

> knowledge only through the *cleansing* that is
> shown must come to those that would be
> saved from the destructions that are given
> there. (281–16)

It is by purification and cleansing of the inner self that man can escape the destruction to his spirit created by selfishness. Only by returning to God can the soul be liberated from the accumulated burdens of earthly lives.

Babylon collapsed under the weight of its own self-indulgence, to fall to Cyrus, a universal liberator. Cyrus gave all the captive nations an opportunity to serve the gods they worshiped.

Israel was presented with a choice. They could remain in Babylon, plying the merchant trade which had made them wealthy, and retain their positions of influence and authority—or they could return to their Holy City, devastated Jerusalem, and build it anew.

Israel had followed the laws of God and accumulated the wealth of the world and knowledge. Now, if they were to continue following God, they must, like the rich young man in Jesus' parable, divest themselves of their earthly attachments. Their earthly ambitions led them into Babylon, a symbol for the egocentric, carnal-minded level of consciousness that holds the soul captive in the earth and its pleasures.

Only a handful, a remnant, stimulated and awakened by the Spirit, went back to Jerusalem to rebuild and complete the purpose which brought the Adamic race into the earth.

This ambition was not for any of man's earthly desires. It was no longer for riches, for the fame and renown of any particular nation, tribe, or individual—but for God alone, for His Spirit and the validation of His promises and protection. The purpose was spiritual, as it had been from the beginning. They were returning to the Holy City, the first ideal, to rediscover and obtain that original and permanent state of consciousness which souls knew before the fall. Jerusalem symbolizes man's effort to rebuild that condition while in the flesh.

THE RESURRECTION

A Cayce reading makes the startling statement that without the resurrection the whole purpose of Jesus' life "would have been as naught." (5749–10) The experience would have counted for nothing. A challenging concept, but true! Many holy men before and after Jesus have preached the kingdom of God and performed great miracles, but none have risen from the dead to be the answer to all man's needs and questions.

The resurrection is equally significant in the Old Testament.

In Ezekiel's famous vision of the dry bones (Ezekiel 37), the Lord was calling His people out of the graveyard of Babylon to the new life in the Promised Land. Unless the spirit could resurrect His people from the spiritual death, the whole purpose, the whole history—and the Bible itself—would have been lost, and the story of men would be incomplete.

In whatever way we may be dying—to whatever degree we may have already died—God's words are clear, "Unless I can restore you to life, I am not the Lord."

> *Then he said to me, Son of man, all these bones are the bones of the children of Israel, who said, Our bones are dried and our hope is lost; we are completely gone.*
>
> *Therefore prophesy and say to them, Thus says the Lord God; Behold, I will open your graves and bring you up out of them and bring you into the land of Israel.*

And you shall know that I am the Lord, when I have opened your graves and brought you up out of them,

And I will put my spirit in you, and you shall live, and I shall place you in your own land; then you shall know that I am the Lord; I have spoken it, and I will do it, says the Lord God. (Ezekiel 37:11–14)

10

Return from Bondage

Evidence is so scarce for this last and most critical, and crucial, phase of the Old Testament history, that one authority writes: "We are in the direst need of information as to the history of the Jews in the Persian period, and every scrap of material that promises help ought to be treasured and put to use."[*]

The two short books of Ezra and Nehemiah are the principal sources of information, and the authenticity of these books is seriously argued by Bible scholars. Most agree that Nehemiah is authentic history, but many dispute all claims to the reliability of Ezra.

The importance of this period is enormous. It is the last important period of revelation and activity between the Old Testament and the birth of Christ. It was the events in the Persian period that led to the restoration of the Jews in the Holy Land, a necessary precondition for the coming of the Christ.

No arguments can be settled until conclusive evidence is uncovered which will be acceptable and "treasured" by scholars. Until then, those who accept the readings as a reliable source of information will have

---

[*]*Interpreter's Bible*, Abingdon Press.

graphic and illuminating insights which confirm, and conform to, the historical outline presented in the Bible, enriched with a lustrous portrayal of personalities, events, issues and controversies.

A surprising amount of the Biblical incarnations in the readings fall into this period. Perhaps this was because of the relative similarity between that period and the present, with the great need to restore and rebuild spiritual ideals in a world threatened to be overrun and overcome with the effects of evil.

PROBLEMS WITH THE READINGS

A large amount of incarnations in the life readings fall into this obscure period and supply considerable details, yet also raise serious questions which may delay their acceptance by scholarly minds. Perhaps the most difficult problem in dealing with their credibility is the consistent view taken that many individuals were active throughout all three returns. It is generally assumed there was a lapse of over one hundred years between the first return under Zerubbabel and the second and third under Ezra and Nehemiah. Thus, orthodox dating would make these individuals well over a century old.

Modern theologians feel that the first return granted by Cyrus was led by Sheshbazzar (Ezra 1:11) and was unsuccessful, and occasioned Zerubbabel's return years later during the reign of Darius. If this assumption is true, then it would put the three returns closer in time and make the "overlapping" expeditions in the readings credible. Yet the readings themselves adhere to the orthodox chronology.

The only way to have a basis to accept the view suggested by the readings of hale and hearty individuals over a century old still engaged in the work of rebuilding Jerusalem is to find an acceptable means to extend the lifespan of these individuals.

The Bible indicates that man's life in the beginning spanned centuries. The life was "nearly a thousand years" and gradually shortened "first from a thousand to a hundred and twenty, then to eighty" because of man's desire for self-gratification. (3976-29) Thus man can reverse the pattern. Our present life-span of seventy years is self-imposed and arbitrary, and can be extended indefinitely by living in harmony with certain creative principles. Dr. Josef P. Hrachovec, an expert on aging at the University of Southern California gerontology center, recently stated that all men have an inborn potential for living a century or longer. Dr. Hrachovec claims proper diet and exercise, and learning how to control emotional pressures, could enable modern man to stretch his life-span "like a rubberband." Another expert, Dr. Roy M. Hamlin, a research psychologist, says that if an individual feels needed and is willing to work, he can and will retain his competence and live longer, up to 120 and 140 years old.

These contemporary insights suggest the possibility of hearty individuals active under the regimes of Zerubbabel, Ezra, and Nehemiah.

The readings also give no support to another popular view growing among Biblical scholars that Nehemiah's return actually preceded Ezra's. The picture created by the readings follows in outline the structure presented in the Bible. Scholars feel there are too many contradictions and unresolved questions in the Ezra-Nehemiah narrative, and in order to reconstruct the true picture, transpose and interpolate chapters from Ezra to Nehemiah and vice versa. The readings fill in many of these questions and seeming contradictions, showing why Nehemiah had to follow Ezra, thus resolving many of the issues and sparing us the necessity of revision.

All the evidence is not in which would validate the readings' descriptions of this obscure Ezra-Nehemiah period, or discount them. But for now it presents a fascinating and complementary picture to that in the Bible, with descriptions of events and issues that will broaden our orthodoxy.

A RELIGION BASED ON THE DICTATES OF CONSCIENCE

The true significance of this return and rebuilding is impossible to contain in definitions. Three of mankind's greatest boons are rooted in this period: the national life and character of the Jew was preserved; it made possible the birth of Christ; and gave us the Bible. Without that handful whose spirit "God had stirred," it is unlikely we would have had any or all of these three. To evaluate what these three events have contributed to man from then to the present is to appraise the significance to this period.

The purpose for the return was stated in a variety of ways in the readings: to rehabilitate a destroyed purpose, a destroyed ideal (257-201); or, as "a definite mission, a definite purpose," by people who were called by God to establish His name in a definite and given place (454-2); and who were to complete the activity that would cause man to take thought of the spiritual forces in the earth. (510-1)

The most frequently stated purpose was to "re-establish a religion based upon the dictates of conscience." (1201-2, 1210-1, 1285-1, 1638-1, 2545-1)

Only by man becoming aware of his own soul can he complete his spiritual evolution. The Israelites kept to their commitment to advance the spiritual understanding of man through the awareness of the inner light, or God-within. Thus, they had to re-establish an approach to God based upon the understanding of the "inner-self" or soul and its relationship to its source.

To prove this concept, they had to put it into application, reconstructing that which had become only "a hearsay to most" (2305–2): They were called to preserve "the tenets of old" and to bring forth that which could create and renew the purposes in the hearts and minds of those that would know their relationship to God. (1825–1)

This is the concept most affecting and influencing us today. Where do we stand in relation to our "conscience," to the prompting of our own souls? Do we honor it, or disregard it? How true are we to our spiritual convictions, and moral insights, and ethical standards? What do we value more than our own personal worth?

By becoming aware of our own souls, the inner light of the divine spark, we will be guided into all manner of truth and to the ultimate realization of who we really are, and what God has implanted within. But the voice of "conscience" must become strong, and obeyed despite all the hardships, turmoil, misunderstanding, and opposition which one will receive while in the earth, staying true to that sure and trustworthy guidance. This is a discernible experience in the rebuilding.

> For His love faileth not to sustain those that put their trust in Him. And though He slay thee, though He break thee as flax upon the wheel, though He bestir thee to the depths of despair, know thy Redeemer liveth—and thou shalt see Him, and He shall purify thee in those things that thou doest that are lovely unto thy fellow man. (378–18)

ADAM REINCARNATED

Jeshua—Leader of the First Return

The final Old Testament incarnation of the soul who had been Adam, Enoch, Melchizedek, Joseph,

Joshua, and Asaph, the readings state, was Jeshua, the high priest who, with Zerubbabel, led the first return, and was responsible for the ecclesiastic leadership in the community and directed the rebuilding of the temple.

Jeshua's name heads the list of those who came with Zerubbabel (Ezra 2:2). He, with the priests and Zerubbabel, rebuilt the altar (Ezra 3:2) and revived the feast of Booths (Ezra 3:4) and all the festivals sacred to the Lord. (Ezra 3:5) (The feast of Booths had been instituted by Joshua and had not been observed since his time. Cayce noted in the Bible class that it was no coincidence that Jeshua revived this feast, since he, as Joshua, had been the one to inaugurate it.)

Jeshua also directed the work on the house of the Lord. (Ezra 3:8). He and Zerubbabel rebuffed the mixture of people when they first attempted to join the work. (Ezra 4:3) He was one who was "stirred up" by Haggai and Zechariah to renew the rebuilding after fifteen years of delay. (Ezra 5:2) Jeshua's sons head Ezra's list of those who had taken foreign wives. (Ezra 10:18) He and his sons also head Nehemiah's list of the interpreters who were able to make the law understood by the people. (Nehemiah 8:7)

The readings add to the accomplishments of Jeshua: He was active in translating, classifying, and codifying the laws, putting them into the language of the people. As a translator, he rewrote the Scripture from Genesis through Nehemiah. Teaching, reading, writing, and translating the law so that it could be acceptable and understood by the learned priests as well as the lowly day laborer, with all the different tongues and dialects the returning Jews brought back to Jerusalem, must have resulted in an enduring development in Jeshua to make himself understood.

With this background, it is easy to see how, in his final incarnation as Jesus, this soul had the ability to astonish the priests as a callow child of twelve, able to draw large masses to him as a man and to renew and revitalize those he had chosen.

As Jeshua, the soul completed that development which enabled him, in his next incarnation, to become the Saviour of man.

The understanding of the Jeshua-Jesus connection also adds new import to Zechariah's visions concerning the high priest.

In its historical setting, this vision in which a heavenly court absolves Jehsua of all iniquity and changes his "filthy garments" for clean apparel signifies the divine sanction for the ecclesiastical authority of the high priest in face of doubts of a returned exile for the office. It also signifies his jurisdiction over the temple.

But what is it also saying about the *soul* of this entity who was so near to that state of purification and perfection which he reached as Jesus the Christ? What does it also say about Zechariah's own awareness (on a different level of consciousness) of the *true* identity of Jeshua?

Zechariah's vision is:

Then he showed me Jeshua the high priest standing before the angel of the Lord, and Satan standing at his right hand to harm him.

And the angel of the Lord said to Satan, The Lord rebuke you, O Satan; even the Lord who has chosen Jerusalem rebuke you. Is not this a brand plucked out of the fire?

Now Jeshua was clothed with filthy garments, and stood before the angel of the Lord.

And the angel answered and spoke to those who stood before him, saying, Take away the filthy garments from him. And to him said, Behold, I have caused your iniquity to pass from you, and I will clothe you with good raiment.

And he said, Let them put a clean mitre on his

head and clothe him with good garments. And the angel of the Lord stood by.

And the angel of the Lord charged Jeshua saying,

Thus says the Lord of hosts: If you will walk in my ways and keep my commandments, then you shall also judge my house and keep my courts, and I will grant you to walk among these that stand by.

Hear now, O Jeshua the high priest, you and your fellows are marvelous men: Behold I will bring forth the rising of the sun upon my servant.

For behold the stone that I have laid before Jeshua; upon one stone shall be seven facets; behold, I will open its gates, says the Lord of hosts, and I will remove the iniquity of that land in that day.

In that day, says the Lord of hosts, every man shall invite his neighbor under the vine and under the fig tree. (Zechariah 3:1-10)

The second vision of Zechariah is fraught with even more significance, both temporal and cosmic, concerning Jeshua's destiny. A coronation is envisioned.

This word of the Lord then came to me: Take from the returned captives Heldai, Tobijah, Jedaiah; and go the same day to the house of Josiah, son of Zephaniah (these had come from Babylon).

Silver and gold you shall take and make a crown; place it on the head of Jeshua, son of Jehosadak, the high priest. And say to him thus says the Lord: Here is a man whose name is Shoot, and where he is he shall sprout, and he shall build the temple of the Lord.

Yes, he shall build the temple of the Lord, and taking up the royal insignia, he shall sit as ruler upon his throne. The priest shall be at his right hand, and between the two of them there shall be friendly understanding.

The crown itself shall be a memorial offering in the temple of the Lord in favor of Heldai, Tobijah, Jedaiah, and the son of Zephaniah. And they who were from afar shall come and build the temple of the Lord, and you shall know that the Lord of hosts has sent me to you. And if you heed carefully the voice of the Lord your God all this shall come to pass." *(Zechariah 6:9–15)*

THE LAST LIFE

As Jeshua, the soul who had been Adam, Enoch, Melchizedek, Joseph, Joshua, and Asaph, collected and organized the many strands of activity he had begun in the earth.

A brief analysis will show how true this statement is, made by Edgar Cayce:

> . . . from the very first of the Old Testament to the very last even of Revelation, He is not merely the subject of the Book, He is the author of the greater part, having given to man the mind and the purpose for its having been put in print. (5322–1)

As Jeshua he aided the people in their return to the original purpose and ideal he had brought with him as Adam. As Enoch, he had given blessings and recommendations (2072–4) and warned against the flood. Thus he insured the preservation of a remnant who were "perfect in their day and generation" and

---

*Slightly amended from The New American Bible (New York: P. J. Kenedy & Sons). A footnote in The New American Bible for this passage points out that Jeshua is not the one crowned in the vision, but the Shoot. This would indicate the Shoot represents the Spirit, or the Christ itself, upon which the crown is to be placed. In his next incarnation, Jesus was that *Shoot.*

whose spiritual and mental advances were leading factors in civilizing mankind. (2627-1) As Melchizedek he had initiated Abraham into God's new plan after the flood. Melchizedek also wrote Job (262-55) and other teachings which were used by Samuel and Elisha to found the School of Prophets (254-109). The prophets kept Israel from being completely destroyed. In Babylon the School of Prophets was discontinued, but revived under Ezra (2444-1) Jeshua must have been instrumental in reactivating the School of Prophets which preserved and practiced the esoteric and mystical concepts given by Melchizedek. The School of Prophets became the Essene sect within Jewry, through which, as the readings show, there came the virgin birth of Jesus.

As Joseph he had preserved his people again; and as Joshua he had conquered and settled the promised land, insuring the place where the divine drama would be staged. Several centuries later they still possessed the arena Joshua had obtained for them.

As Asaph he had been in charge during the days of David, and founded the guild of Levitical singers and musicians who lifted the people's consciousness with praise and thanksgiving. As Jeshua led the people in the effort to rebuild and restore their way of life, he was aided by the sons of Asaph (Ezra 3:10), musicians skilled in attuning the minds of the people to spirit within.

As Jeshua, the entity interpreted, translated, and rewrote the whole Bible as it had been lived and recorded since the beginning.

All the strands, the threads, were gathered together, and Jeshua was responsible for organizing and collecting them, putting them into a working whole.

The people he had been leading and serving had passed through the experiences of the world. They had been tested, strengthened, purified, chastened, and purged. They were returning back to God and to a service in His name. Jeshua had passed through it all with them.

All that remained was the final return as David's heir—the Saviour.

11

The First Return

Zerubbabel and Jeshua were the leaders of the first return. Zerubbabel was appointed by Cyrus as governor of Judah. Although Zerubbabel is generally considered to be a direct descendant of David, the readings describe him as a priest, which would make him a Levite and not of the household of Judah. Perhaps Cyrus was more willing to trust a priest than a former member of the old ruling family. Cyrus did appoint one of Zedekiah's direct descendants as a record keeper and gave him a place in the first return. (See 1120–1)

Because so little is known of this period outside the Bible, the rebuilding is said to be a monument to the anonymous individuals, the forgotten men and women who worked, amid so many dangers and hardships, to reconstruct that which had been lost, which was to be the hope, the light of the world.

Zerubbabel, Jeshua, and 42,360 Jews, 7,337 servants, and 200 singers, with 5,400 vessels of gold and silver, set out across a forbidding and hostile terrain to resettle their devastated and depopulated homeland.

The contribution they made is unrivaled. Through the life readings we are given valuable glimpses of their story.

A reading for a ten-year-old boy tells of his experience as an interpreter of the spiritual and mental motivations of the Jews as they set out on "that unusual journey" from Babylon to Jerusalem:

> Before that the entity was in the Persian land when there were those edicts by the individuals in authority, when there was the allowing of the peoples of the Holy Land to return and build the city and the temple.
>
> The entity was among those given authority to aid with those peoples active in their return. Thus the entity, it might be said, was the one given authority by the Persian king to go with Zerubbabel and those peoples, as they prepared for that unusual journey.
>
> Thus again we see reasons for the interpreting in the entity's experience of those lands, in this particular sojourn.
>
> The entity aided much, and the interpretation of those promptings of the spiritual as well as the mental laws through that period made for developments in those forces that will be the greater urges in this particular experience.
>
> The name then was Zeldezer. (2890-2)

Many of the prophecies throughout the Bible can only be realized and fulfilled through a search for, and love of, God. Jeremiah had prophesied, in the name of the Lord, ". . . I will give them a heart to know me . . . and they shall be my people and I shall be their God when they return to me with their whole heart." (Jeremiah 24:7) Now the time was fulfilled.

This reading speaks of that determination.

In April, 1931, an eleven-year-old girl was told:

> The entity was then among those of the first peoples to return, during that period when Zerubbabel led the peoples back again. Little

thought, little care, little attention was taken by those people in that land as to whether foes were without or within, but with an eye-single to return to a service of a one source, and one force, was uppermost in the minds of those who journeyed; and the entity was as a companion to those of the priests that led the peoples back—not the high priest, but those of the priests' household and in those of the ones that were the enterers into the outer courts in the new established forces. The entity gained through this experience, in the name Pleneheai . . . for trained in the beginning, added to by precept and example, the entity served in bringing aid, succor, counsel, understanding, to those in the way—and in the re-established homes. (2668–1)

Perhaps the second return under Ezra was even more unusual than the first under Zerubbabel. Ezra was a great reformer who was "ashamed" to ask for a Persian military escort. He felt God's protection was sufficient and should be impressed upon the people. Thus he passed through the same hostile territory with great treasures, armed only with his trust in God.

An experience as a guide and hunter for those of the first return was recalled by Edgar Cayce in this reading:

There the entity was active as an aid to Zerubbabel; not as a priest but rather as a guide. For the entity had been a hunter and thus aided in carrying on those activities through even hostile lands when the great amount of booty or of things had to be cared for in order to make the various offices of the priest become again effective. The entity acted in the capacity of taking care of these. (3268–1)

A Jewish writer and housewife was told she had been a daughter of Zerubbabel. The reading mentions Ur, which reminds us that land of captivity was the same land from which Abraham had been called and sounds a note, again, about the purpose of the return:

> ... we find [the entity] in that land when there was the return from the wanderings, and the walls of the temple were rebuilt, and as Zerubbabel led the peoples from the Ur and from the Chaldean country—the entity among those that made for the *betterment* of the understanding influences of the peoples as a chosen peoples, as a people with a definite mission, a definite purpose, called of the Divine to establish the name in a given place, a given purpose, to a *waiting* world. In the experience, many hardships. In the name Zephaniah, and the daughter of Zerubbabel, the entity led many to a better understanding of *God's*—Jehovah's—relationship to His people; making much, then, of the hangings of the new temple, and especially brocades have a peculiar fascination to the entity from this experience; and blue and gold are the colors the entity seeks to find often in their varying shades—as does the pomegranate, and the hangings of gold in pomegranate folds, make for an interesting thing to be handled by the entity ...
>
> *Write* of self in Jerusalem, and it will be a masterpiece! Take this as the basis, when a people *cried* unto their God in Chaldea—even in the *abundance* of the land, and in the aid as came through the little things; of a bewildered people, raised to power—and self, with the pater, or father, led those again into the land of desolation, and raised up the temple and its court, and its hangings. A

beautiful—wonderful—condition! Self will lose self easily in this. (454-2)

A Jewish woman from New York was told that as Zerubbabel's niece she had been a strong entity whose ability to bring order out of chaos made her beloved among her people. Cayce, again, reiterates the purpose for the return:

> Before this we find the entity in that land now known as the Persian or Indian, but rather then the Chaldean or Assyrian land, when a peoples were in exile from their promised land, and when there were made those overtures to those in power that there might be the return of these peoples to their native land, and to those activities that were to cause—and that have caused—thought of the spiritual activity in the earth.
> The entity, as a niece to Zerubbabel, in the name Iexlia, gained in favor, gained in power, not only with the rulers in the Chaldean land but in the counsel that was given to those that—with the Zerubbabel and the high priest's command—brought those peoples into the promised land; aiding in setting to work those as the classifications of their own abilities in the various fields of activity necessary in that land, bringing order out of chaos in the eyes and in the minds of many; and thus in the physical experience endearing self to those that were to again carry on to that whereunto a peoples had been called in a manner to present in the experiences of their lives their concept of the Creative Forces in their experience . . .
> In the present the concepts of authority are founded most upon that *innately* gained in that sojourn, yet at the same time making

for the appreciations of the activities of others
that in their own development must meet
their *own* problems. (510–1)

Another Jewish woman, a thirty-eight-year-old
widow, was told that, like her forefathers in the Exodus,
she was torn between the comforts of captivity and
the hardships which come while earning freedom.

Before that the entity was in the Promised Land, during that period when there
was the returning to the rebuilding of the
temple, the re-establishing of the faith of the
fathers in the land.
The changes that were wrought brought
into the experience of the entity the hardships,
the longings for things as they had been and
as they might be under the varying circumstances, or as before they had been separated
from the worldly aspects to consider the spiritual future of its peoples.
But in service—as the entity established
with the daughters of Zerubbabel, or as one
of them—in the name Abijah—the entity
gained materially, mentally, spiritually.
So may the entity gain in this present
experience, in the re-establishing of self in
those ways which are not past finding out.
For, those who search to know may find
Him. (2401–1)

ALTARS AND THE HOME

... the highest of man's achievement in the
earth—the *HOME!* (480–20)

... the home is the nearest pattern in earth
(where there is unity of purpose in the com-
panionship) to man's relationship to his Mak-

er. For it is ever creative in purpose from personalities and individualities coordinated for a cause, an ideal. (3577–1)

Zerubbabel's chief mission was to resettle the homeland and re-establish the way of life which would allow the expression of the deepest spiritual instincts of his people.

He began the reconstruction of the temple building and revived the priesthood. Another important effort was directed toward the home life and the family unit, especially the children.

The love of family has been one of the strongest elements in Judaism since the time of Abraham.* Thus, as the Jews returned to their devastated city, re-establishing homes and home life became a concern of the first order. The family was the basic unit which would insure survival and continuity of purpose.

Home altars, as symbols and reminders of sacrifice and devotion to God, were considered a necessary part of every home, as this entity was told in her reading:

> . . . when the edicts of the king in the Persian land made it possible for the return of the children of promise to the Holy Land . . .
>
> We find the entity was among those who came with the earlier portion, or under Zerubbabel. And while there were periods of turmoil, periods of anxiety, there was builded the greater service in the temple and its activities—in the closer associations with those who would establish the home first, as might be called, or the altar in the home.
>
> And these brought into the experience

---

*A thorough presentation of the philosophy in the Edgar Cayce readings regarding home and marriage is given in *Marriage and the Home* (Virginia Beach, Va.: A.R.E. Press).

of the entity then, as Shumel, the great abilities of creative forces as to the establishing of home, the establishing of associations with others in their aids to build better environments for children, for the teaching of others for activity in individual service—as in vocational training and activities. (1872–1)

This entity, born in captivity, found deep meanings in the home, an answering to the longings of the soul.

The entity was among the first of the peoples that came again under Zerubbabel to the Holy City, and of that people; though, to be sure, was born in exile.

Home—home—has become as a portion of the entity's experience that is latent and finds ever and anon the expression of same in the desires of the inner self to see or to know, to feel the security of some place, some surrounding in which that may be felt as a part of the whole self.

Not so much as the religious thought or purposes during the experience, for the ENTITY was rather interested in the purposes for freedom!

And this is a portion of the entity's experience in the present . . . .

Then the name was Judith. (1082–3)

A Protestant housewife was told that as Zerubbabel's daughter-in-law, she had made impressive contributions for the welfare of the children:

Before that the entity was in those activities when there was the returning of the children of promise to the Holy Land; when there were the preparations for the renewing of the service in the temple.

It was when there was the re-establishing of those activities there under Zerubbabel and Ezra and Nehemiah. All of these were acquaintances of the entity, but Zerubbabel was the closer relationship, for the entity was his daughter-in-law.

The name then was Jephtha. In the experience the entity set the example for the mothers in that period, by the establishing—in the homes of those who returned to the city—the teaching centers for the children, for the making known of the awareness of the law as well as the ordinances, as well as the (meanings of those things which had) been established by Aaron and Moses and the earlier priests . . . (910–4)

Home life is mentioned again in the experience of this outstanding life:

. . . as Zerubbabel set out for the long journey again to the city in the hills there in Jerusalem, the entity was among those of that company; and with the entering in aided in the setting of the home life again to the ordinances of the homes as of old . . . and the entity aided much in giving to those peoples an understanding in the preserving of that *innate* in her peoples as to the *necessity*— in the material law as well as in the moral law—of preserving of self in cleanliness as well as in godliness; the preserving not only of the letter of the law but the spirit of the law. And truly, indeed, it may be said of the entity then, as Ashai, that the people under her aid builded with a *will;* for they *minded* the things that pertained to God.

In the experience the entity gained throughout; though there were hardships of travel, though there were hardships of privation during the early portions of the experience. Yet in the latter portion there was not only the satisfaction of seeing the restoring of the worship in the city and in the temple, but the satisfaction of seeing her own peoples raised to places of accomplishments in the affairs pertaining to the king and the city again established there.

There comes to the entity in the present, in the periods of the deeper meditation, those things that take hold upon the offices pertaining to temple service. These have at times been ruthlessly trod upon by others; and it has brought in the experience of the entity much that has made for a longing and a loneliness deep within. (872–1)

THE GREAT CONFLICT

Religious differences are the swords of men. Man's evolution in the earth is to bring him to the understanding that he is his brother's keeper. That consciousness is absolute, eternal, unchanging, and without beginning or end. "Thou shalt love the Lord thy God, with thy whole heart and mind, and thy neighbor as thyself" is not only a commandment, but it is the spirit of God Himself, which, when applied and understood, makes man one with Him.

No matter what our backgrounds and past may be, all must eventually realize our oneness with God and our fellow man.

But—

. . . more wars, more bloodshed have been shed over the racial and religious differences than over any other problem! These, too, must go the way of all others; and man must learn—if he will know the peace as promised by Him—that God loveth those who love Him, whether they be called of this or that sect or schism or ism or cult! The Lord is *One!* (3976-27)

Not all the 42,000 Jews who went with Zerubbabel followed him to Jerusalem. Many settled in cities along the way, or returned to their ancestral home sites. Only a small number actually settled in Jerusalem to begin the work.

In the seventh month of the first year, Jeshua and Zerubbabel summoned the people from all their settlements to gather in the Holy City for the dedication of the altar. (Ezra 3:1)

The next milestone was the laying of the foundation for the temple. This was accomplished in the second month of the second year, and occasioned another memorable celebration.

> *. . . the priests stood up in their vestments with trumpets of rams blowing with them, and the Levites, the sons of Asaph with large trumpets, to praise the Lord according to the ordinance of David, king of Israel.*
>
> *And they sang and praised in unison, giving thanks to the Lord for he is good . . . And all the people shouted with a great shout when they praised the Lord because the foundation of the house of the Lord was laid. (Ezra 3:10–11)*

The beginning of the work was promising, but as it progressed it attracted the attention of the "outsiders," and the great problem which characterizes this whole period began—strife created from racial and religious differences, the "great conflict" found most frequently in the history of man.

The "outsiders" are those ever-present people who

don't think like we do, who are of a different race or cult or creed, who have different problems and needs from ours. The "outsiders" are everywhere, omnipresent, and found on every pathway that leads us back to God.

The "outsiders" in this case were the mixture of people who were the result of the intermarriage between the Jews who were left in the land and the settlers imported by the Assyrian and Babylonian kings. (See 2 Kings 17:24–31)

The Assyrian king had allowed the foreigners he brought to Palestine to be instructed by Jewish priests, so the new residents would be familiar with the local god. As a result of their instruction and intermarriage, the mixed people recognized Jehovah, but also worshiped their own idols. Thus they were not "pure" in their religion.

Intermarriage was forbidden in the law of Moses, and the reformers returning from Babylon were intent upon establishing the pure form of their traditional religion.

The mixed people desired to join in with the work, which they considered a part of their heritage, but were refused.

> *But Zerubbabel and Jeshua and the rest of the chiefs of the fathers of Israel said to them, You have nothing to do with us to build a house to our God; for we ourselves together will build a house to the Lord God of Israel, as Cyrus, king of Persia, commanded us. (Ezra 4:3)*

The mixture people had enjoyed privilege and position under the Assyrian and neo-Babylonian regimes, but now that the Persians controlled the territory, their circumstances were changed. The Jews promised to be the new ruling class under the Persians. Perhaps it was the political rather than the religious factors which motivated the mixture people to join with

the Jews, and inspired the rebuff from Jeshua and Zerubbabel.

Whatever the cause of the rejection, the results
were predictable—resentment and hostility.

> *Then the Gentiles of the land weakened the hands*
> *of the people of Judah, and terrified them that*
> *they should not build, and hired objectors against*
> *them to frustrate their purpose all the days of*
> *Cyrus king of Persia, even until the reign of Darius.*
> *(Ezra 4:5)*

As time progressed, the emotional climate intensified. Because of their efforts to frustrate the purposes of
the Jews by blocking their efforts to rebuild, the mixture people—later known as the Samaritans—became
hated and mistrusted with an intensity that endured to
the time of Jesus, four hundred years later.

Any opportunity for large-scale unity was destroyed. The divisions and differences between the two
groups became set and settled into hard and durable
molds. And out of the fracture came a new group, a
new denomination, a distinct people, a separate nation
—another label—*Samaritan*—to separate men.

The Samaritans remained well-versed in the law of
Moses and the prophets, but differed in their interpretations. They kept to the days, the seasons, and the
moons of Jewish law. The real dividing factor was the
place chosen for worship. (993–5) They chose as their
holy place the mountain where Jeroboam had established his altar. (1 Kings 12:23, 29; 262–9)

As the readings state, the most important factor
in worship is not the place, the name, or any other
external forms in the way you worship. The most
important factor is the purpose of the heart. This deter-
mines whether your religion is constructive or destructive. Israel is not a physical nation, but a spiritual
pattern and consciousness. True religion should not be

limiting and exclusive, but all-embracing and encompassing.

Many of the mixed people were sincere in their purposes, while many among the Jews were misguided in their judgments.

The life readings show a deteriorating relationship between the mixed people and the Jews which intensified as the rebuilding continued.

This reading suggests the existence of a friendly climate in the earliest days of the rebuilding.

A Massachusetts man was told:

> There we find the entity was with Zerubbabel and those peoples returning to the Holy City.
>
> The entity made for friendships with many of the natives and with the conditions surrounding, in the name then Abjadel; being in associations with those in authority, being in connection with those put in places of confidence and hope.
>
> Yet the entity held not altogether to those tenets, and there came a period through which much disturbance arose owing to the conditions and hardships that were brought about.
>
> Meet them then in the present, in the way in which the greater promise may be fulfilled—"If ye will abide with me I will abide with thee."
>
> And remember the new commandment, "Love one another." Not in a possessive manner. O that all would learn that LOVE is all-embracing, and NOT merely possession! (1816–1)

An English chiropractor and naturopath was told of her experience as one of the mixture people. She worked in the spirit that would unite the diverse elements.

> ... the entity was among those peoples that had been left in the land when there were the activities in the exodus of the main body, or of that peoples.

> For the period covered years and years. Yet when there were those activities under the supervision of Zerubbabel, the priest, and Nehemiah and Ezra, the lawgiver and the priest and the active service, the entity persuaded many of her own peoples—that were called later the mixed races, or the peoples that were hated later by their own brethren—to become closer affiliated, closer associated with the spiritual activity in the lives of the individuals.

> Thus the entity builded in that experience not only in the material but in the mental and the spiritual activities.

> Thus may the entity build in the experiences of others in all the various thoughts in which the entity has delved and thus contact not the differences but rather that which is co-ordinant in the principles, the teachings of many varied sects and activities of others.

> These are a part of the entity's experience in the present in contacting many that are of various faiths, of various cults, of various beliefs, or various tenets.

> These, then, if the entity will find that common ground upon which all may meet for a *goodly* purpose, will be as the experience of the entity then—in the name Shulmean, which made for that development mentally, spiritually, materially. (1397–1)

An English welfare investigator was told she had struck the note that led to class and caste distinctions between the two groups.

> Before that we find the entity was in the land now called the promised land, during the periods of the returning of the children of promise from the Chaldean land.
> There we find the entity was among those peoples who came with Zerubbabel, and of those who aided in extending the activities to help others.
> The entity was among those who refused its own brethren (though of a different cult in the experience) from joining; and thus making for periods when there was too great a consideration of class or the acknowledgement of all being of one purpose.
> The name then was Hannah. In the experience the entity gained, the entity lost and lost; gaining in the abilities to meet the circumstances which arose; losing in forming too great a class distinction and producing great hatred during those experiences . . .
> Hence in the present we find that the greater service may be in aiding those who are as new arrivals in a strange land, or enabling individuals to become acquainted with or accustomed to new surroundings and new environs, as well as enabling those of every nation and every tongue to meet upon a common ground of service to ONE God. (1897–1)

This individual, as a priest and an authority, worked to establish better relationship between all groups, so that distinctions between class, race or office would be minimized.

The entity was in the authority of the builders, yet given in service for the preparing and the attending of the sacrifices that were prepared during those experiences.

Hence a priest, and of the household of the Levites—and a close association with Zerubbabel, though not of the same house—in the name then Zepheniath.

In the experience the entity made for closer associations with those that were in the agricultural activities, with those that were as the merchants and the tradesmen; and these made for the great stresses that were brought upon the activities of the entity in associations with those that were left in the land aforetime when there was the carrying away to captivity. But the entity made for the better relationships, and these give the abilities for the making of closer relationships and closer undertakings between the laborers and those in authority. (1442–1)

THE WORK STOPS

Cyrus was seldom home to personally hear and settle the disputes and intrigue in the courts between the Jews and their adversaries. He was spreading his empire in other parts of the world until, in 530 B.C., he was slain in battle. Cambyses had been appointed by Cyrus as regent of Babylon. With Cyrus' death, Cambyses became king. He ordered all work on the temple and the walls around the city stopped, and dispatched a large army to see that his edicts were obeyed.

The Jews actually made very little progress on the temple or the refortifications of the city for over one hundred years. When the temple was built, the elders, who had seen the original temple structure, wept over its insignificance. Whenever the Jews would start to work on the wall, their more powerful neighbors would either bluff them off by force, or intrigue to get orders from the Persian court to halt the work.

Cambyses' order led to a fifteen-year shutdown on all the rebuilding, during which time the Jews were confronted with dangers and hardships from hostile neighbors.

Application of spiritual lessons in this trying time led to a greater vision for this woman:

> Before that we find that the entity was in the land when there were those returning from captivity to the Holy Land.
>
> There the entity was of those peoples who came with Zerubbabel, and among those in authority; being the companion or wife of one who served in the holy temple in that experience.
>
> Thus we find that the entity was among those bearing the hardships of material activities, yet enabling such to give to the generations of that experience, as well as to those to follow, the greater concept of the relationship of man to the Creative Forces, and how that such activities are reflected in the influence or force which directs the individual in the relationships to the fellow man, as well as to the ritualistic forces combined in the services throughout the activities in the holy temple and holy activities . . .
>
> The name then was Susannah. (2054-2)

Afraid of their opponents and blocked by legal sanctions and political forces, the work did not advance until Haggai and Zechariah began to stir up the spirit in the people with prophesy. Inspired and exhorted by the two prophets, Jeshua and the people began to labor again. They took the first step, knowing it was the right one, but not always sure where the next was going to lead.

Haggai and Zechariah not only preached but labored. They continued working in spite of the opposition and threats by the neighboring people and government officials who came to question them on their rights.

The dispute grew and went up to higher and higher levels of government as the Jews persisted in building, until finally the matter reached the court of Darius, the new king of Persia.

To settle the complex issues, Darius ordered a search for Cyrus' decree which gave authority to the Jews. Darius is remembered by historians as a great administrator, and the Persians were famous as record keepers. The original decree was found. When it was discovered, Darius ordered that nothing should stand in the way of the work. He also decreed—and this was a bitter reversal for the Gentiles—that the expenses of the reconstruction be taken out of the tribute and taxes he received from that area. The opponents were going to finance the work they had opposed! Anyone who frustrated these purposes, Darius decreed, would be put to death! (Ezra 5, 6)

As the readings so often and well advised, "Take the first step, and the next will be given." Or, as Edgar Cayce told his Bible class, if we listen and hold to what we believe, and disregard what others may say, God will provide a way. By taking the first step and resuming the work, the way opened, which not only allowed the temple to be completed but brought unexpected benefits in royal patronage and support.

One of the prophecies of Haggai, which encouraged and stregthened the heart of the people, was interpreted in the readings:

Q-5. Please explain Haggai 2:7, "And I will shake all nations and the desire of all nations shall come; and I will fill this house with glory, saith the Lord of hosts."

A–5. In the interpretation of that spoken by Haggai or any of the prophets, take into consideration first to whom the message was being given. Yet know that any message that bespeaks God's dwelling in the heart or in the temple of man is to the individual a lesson now, today. Here we find, however, from the literal interpretation, that a wayward people had forsaken their temple worship, where they had been appointed to meet with the living God. For there alone they had heard the words, and there alone they had received the instructions as of old. And the interpretation was that these should be turned again, as they were only a few years later, in how that even those that were called the heathen were shaken to the core and *granted* the people again to establish the desire of their heart in rebuilding the temple. As ye have received from Him, "The day cometh when neither in Jerusalem nor in this mountain shall ye seek or desire to know the Lord, for ye will find Him in thine own heart, in thine own conscience; and if the desire of thy heart will be that the temple of thy soul (the image of thy Maker; the soul—not the body—the image of thy Maker) shall be renewed in Him, thou shalt be able in self to know that . . . and the *way* that thou shouldst go." (262–64)

Several life readings give us examples of individuals who helped soften or "shake" the heart of the kings of Persia. In this reading we find a peacemaker and an advocate for the Jews:

Under the leadership of Zerubbabel did the entity return to the Holy City. And as there were those attempts to rebuild the temple and the walls, we find the king called on the entity to act in the capacity as a mediator between the peoples of that individual land and those who had returned for the re-establishing of the land.

Hence we find the entity made overtures to those of the land.

In the present we find abilities from that sojourn; for with Nehemiah, Ezra, and the rest of those in authority, the entity—as Zerubbabel—made for much help and strengthening during those turmoils that were brought by those because of the refusal of the priests to join with the Samaritans in that labor.

Hence we find the entity in the present is inclined to oft be in the midst of turmoils in secular natures pertaining to truths that bear rather upon the individual and those of a city, of a nation, a people, as to what must be the final outcome of their activities.

Know, here again, as in those experiences, there must be the turning to the universal law and not to those of such a secular nature that the individual rather than the masses would be considered.

Hold fast then to ideals that are a part of every soul's development.

AGAIN we find the entity being fitted to deal with conditions in which buildings, as pertain to many natures, become a part of the experience. (1797–1)

In this we find a Persian who favored the persecuted peoples and acted as a go-between in the royal court:

Before that we find the entity was in that land now known as the Persian, during those periods when there were the activities of those peoples who had brought the Jewish people under bondage.

The entity, though of the Persians, was rather inclined towards the persecuted peoples, because of the associations with some of those in those activities; for the entity then married a Jewess!

This, to be sure, brought disturbing experiences, yet the abilities of the entity to later act in the capacity of an interpreter of and for Zerubbabel; as well as becoming closely associated with Nehemiah brought not only the places of responsibility but of judgments necessary in aiding those peoples when they began their return to the Holy Land.

Hence we find the entity acting in those capacities as among the helpers to those persecuted.

In the present we will find the entity will become the defender always of those who are persecuted, or any that might be called the "underdog."

Thus we find that innate need for the manifestation more of, "If you would have friends, be friendly; if you would find love, love your fellow man."

Remember the greater commandment as given by Him, who is Lord of Lords and King of Kings, "Love ye one another, even as I have loved you."

The name then was Eleaza. (2030–1)

OTHER CONFLICTS

In addition to the problems with the "outside" groups, the Jews became divided by conflicts within their own ranks. Questions arose concerning the amount of taxation and who should pay; problems between laborers and those in authority grew up, and class and caste distinctions began. The conflicts were inner in nature, stemming from selfish motives at war with constructive ideals.

This entity, a Russian Jew, was told he had experienced an inner conflict in those days as the desire for earthly gain warred with his spiritual instincts:

> The entity then was among those peoples who aided in the first upbuilding of the temple activity. And many of those things that became as of hearsay, as of tradition, as of the gatherings of those things that made for the activities as they were renewed, came through the hands of the entity then—in the name Adajar.
>
> In the experience the entity gained; and the entity lost when those things that were turned into that for self-indulgence were such that privileges were sold to individuals for conveniences and satisfying of forces within self—these eventually brought destructive forces in the experience.
>
> Hence we may find in the experiences of the entity in the present those periods when duty and the religion, earthly gains and the law of the innate self, clash. But hold fast to that which is the law of One, that ye may know in truth—as has been given—that house, that temple, that soul that finds itself divided against itself becomes one of turmoil. And what gaineth a man though he gain the whole world in fame or fortune and hath lost his own rest, his own peace, his own soul? (1232–1)

A young Jewish student was warned that her spiritual growth had been retarded in past lives by predominant carnal desires. The source of the problem began in Jerusalem:

> The entity then among those who assisted in setting up the temple worship for the peoples, and the entity gained in that experience through the application of self in and for the benefit of many, yet losing in turning same to that of the selfish motive of over loving in the flesh. In the name then Abidiha, and the entity finds the urge, as is seen in the present, of having the ability to keep those who would make love afar, unless the entity desires the use of the individual. This may be used to excess, and to entity's undoing. Beware of same. (480-1)

This reading describes the conflict of a priest torn between selfless service and self-indulgence. He lost his battle and discredited not only himself but the office of the priesthood as well.

A young Jewish merchant was told:

> There we find the entity was among the priests of Zerubbabel, in the name Eljah. In the experience the entity gained, the entity lost. When the activities were such as to make for the greater developments for the whole peoples, well. When there was the use of the office as well as the social affiliations turned into self-indulgence, these brought periods of debasement—not only of self but of the office itself.
>
> And remember, these are but experiences that must be met in thine own self. For an individual through varied experiences in the earth is constantly meeting himself.
>
> Those abilities as an interior decorator,

those abilities to choose hangings for draperies or the like, are innate from those experiences—as are the mental urges to DOUBT—because of self's own abilities to analyze others and their emotions. This does not indicate, because the emotions of an individual may be analyzed, that the individual's real purpose or desire is as open as a book—even to one so gifted as self in the interpretations of the emotions of others.

Use these abilities, then, as well as the indications given, for a greater spiritual awakening, that the material and mental purposes may arise from the results accomplished within self and self's own development, THROUGH the aid to others.

For, know, ever: What ye are speaks so loud, seldom is there heard what ye say. (1950-1)

Here we find conflicting emotions warring within a musician. A young Jewish boy was told, following his experience as a rebel in the Exodus, he had incarnated in Jerusalem:

Before that we find the entity was in the days when there was the rebuilding of the walls of the Holy City, when Nehemiah and Ezra returned to the Holy Land.

The entity was among those who were of the trumpeters about the wall, as well as for the announcing and calling of those for service as defenders as well as those that ministered justice to the peoples during those periods.

There we find the entity gained and lost, and gained; gained when the application of self was in those fields of service for the greater good of all; lost when in the activities self-indulgence and self-aggrandizement became the order of self's relationships with others.

Hence the warnings again that may be given regarding music, as well as its relationships especially to those of the opposite sex. (1881–1)

12

The Second Return

The temple was completed and dedicated in the sixth year of Darius, who had authorized its building.

It is interesting to note that Darius is considered to be the one who established Zoroastrianism as the state religion of Persia. Zoroaster emphasized in his teachings the individuality of man and his responsibility toward the universe in which he lived. The religion stressed moral dualism, that the *Good* God created everything true, wholesome, positive, and constructive while all that is false, immoral, and ugly was the work of the Evil Being. Men must choose to ally themselves with either good or evil, and in the after life would be rewarded in heaven or hell according to their actions on earth. Zoroaster saw that good would ultimately triumph over evil, but the task rested with man and depended upon his will and resources. The one great command of Zoroaster was that man must fight for good.

Perhaps Darius saw the *Good* God working through the Jews, and with this in mind, gave his patronage and support to their effort.

The readings indicate his successor, Xerxes, was

equally absorbed in the events of Jerusalem. This reading suggests why:

> The entity may be said to have been the counselor then to the king, Xerxes; that there might be not only the satisfying of the king's longings for knowledge but that there might be tried out the experiment that those people might proclaim again that which was a portion of their traditions during those experiences. (1297-1)

Esther

Xerxes succeeded Darius as king over the empire, and during his reign Esther became queen. Esther's enthronement occurred around 478 B.C., approximately twenty years before Ezra returned with the second expedition to Jerusalem.

The Book of Esther, many scholars feel, is unhistorical because no records outside the Bible have ever been discovered which confirm the story. According to the Bible, had it not been for Esther and her kinsman Mordecai the Jewish nation would have been completely annihilated 500 years before Christ. If one accepts the Biblical version, Esther is not just a moral tale but a description of a very important event in a crucial epoch of Israel's history.

The readings indicate Esther is based on historical fact. Three principals from the Book of Esther are found among the life readings—Queen Esther herself (1298), Queen Vashti (1096), who is a central figure in the opening chapter, and Haman (1273), who, as the king's prime minister, allegedly plotted the genocide of the Jews (Esther 3:6) and was hung on the gallows he prepared for Mordecai. (Esther 7:10)

The Cayce readings agree in general outline with the story presented in the Bible, but differ in emphasis.

As Cayce told his Bible class:

"We must remember the book of Esther was written by a Jew, so we have only the Jewish side presented."

A beautiful divorcee was told in her reading that she had been Vashti, Ahasuerus' queen, and was advised to write a book about that incarnation. She was told to analyze the Book of Esther, and then "give that of Vashti's version." (1096-1)

The woman obtained three additional readings, rich in historical detail, to secure material for her book. The second in the series supplies background information leading up to the banquet and Vashti's dethronement. (Esther 1)

The reading tells us that with the liberal policies of the Persian kings and their interest in their conquered peoples, there was a great deal of freedom and activity in the royal court among the nationals to secure favored positions with the king. Vashti was an adherent of Zoroastrianism, and represented the regions near India. In the political manipulations and maneuvering, the Jews made an issue of the fact that Vashti was without children, and used it as a means to oust her from the throne.

As there came the experience that Vashti failed in becoming the mother, as had been expected for those activities that were to keep the house or the sons of Ahasuerus upon the throne, then there became more and more the cries from the Jewish peoples that were in the court as counselors or as reporters of the activities that dealt with the service and the actions of those peoples.

More and more came the insinuations of the lack of the interests on the part of those that were in authority in the relatives or relations of Vashti, through the periods of the wars with those in both the northern and in the southern lands, or in the southeastern lands, that *had* brought more and more of the turmoils of a religious thought. (1096–2)

To counteract this, Vashti turned to Haman. The reading continues:

Hence there arose to power, through the activities of Vashti, that one indicated in some records as Haman; and there began then the activities through this as an individual to change the thought, to change the ideals, to change the ideas of the king as respecting these. And yet there was still the harkening of the king to those that made the declamations that no heir was upon the throne. (1096–2)

In the opening chapter of Esther a great feast is described. The drinking and the revelry was uninhibited and unrestrained. There was no ban on the amount one could drink. It was the king's command that everyone should do "according to his pleasure."

Ahasuerus came to the throne in the early twenties, and was not an uncouth man; yet—with the ease of the conditions and surroundings—being lauded by the princes of the various charges over which the counselors came —he became rather what would be termed in the present as a dissipated man. (1096–3)

After seven days of self-indulgence, the king commanded his eunuchs to bring Vashti before his guests to show off her beauty.

But Vashti did the unexpected and unpardonable —she refused! The king, who considered himself a god whose orders were never to be questioned, "was very wroth and his anger burned within him." The princes at the feast argued that not only was the king offended, but they and all the people as well, for the queen had set an example of disobedience to her husband. Lest their own authority be held in contempt, the princes insisted Vashti be deposed. The king obliged and a new queen was selected.

And there were those periods of the abuse of self [the king], in the drunkenness, the dissipations in the activities by those influences not only from the Indian land but from the Jews and those that had attempted to make for those periods of the changing of the king's ideas.

Hence Vashti was *ordered*, not by her own but by the *Jewish* people, to appear at the banquets to display *bodily* charms—as were those of the Jews, and those of the Indians in their dance at the court.

With the refusal of Vashti (and this was only in the early portion of the twenties—in age—of Vashti), then there came the choosing of those that were to take the place of the queen.*

Hence we find, as would be termed in the present day, there was *proclaimed* a

_____
*All time is *one* time, the readings tell us, and the patterns of our past lives continue in the present. We are continually reliving the same experience until new spiritual patterns are established. Mrs. 1096, who was very attractive and appeared much younger than her years, related that she had been married twice and divorced once. Her first marriage was to a well-known real-estate developer whom she felt had been Ahasuerus (Xerxes), since the cause of their divorce came through his insistence that she appear nude before his guests at a large party.

Her second husband was told in his reading that he had been Haman.

beauty pageant of the young women of the land. (1096-2)

If it was not the overt intention of the Jews to have the deposed queen replaced by a Jewess, it became the result. Esther was chosen from among all the beauties of the empire to be Ahasuerus' new queen.

So Esther entered before King Ahasuerus into his royal house . . . And the king loved Esther more than all the other women, and she obtained grace and favor in his sight more than all the other virgins; so that he set the royal crown upon her head and made her queen instead of Vashti. (Esther 2:16-17)

Queen Esther

When another beauty, a career woman and student of metaphysical thought, requested a life reading, an incarnation as Esther was given. The advances made in that life were described as well as the sacrifices.

The entity then was Esther to Ahasuerus, close with those activities that have made for that upon which a peoples have worshiped not the individual but the purposes as wrought in the heart and activities of an individual, as directed by a man of God—Mordecai!

These brought in the experience of the entity the closer concept of the ideals, and yet the very act and fact that the entity itself enjoyed not those privileges of seeing the re-establishing of the temple, or the peace offerings to the inner self before those altars, brought longings and dreads in the experience of the entity—that find in the present that longing for an expression in some manner in which the application of that which has been gained may be the more individual and *not* so much national—yet national in its scope; which may be brought by the entity's application, as was done in those periods—by its writings of that which prompted those beseechings that a people be allowed to worship according to the dictates of their own conscience. For there the entity learned *tolerance,* which so few possess in *any* experience in the earth!

Selflessness is the greater tolerance. For when self seeks exaltation, beware! (1298–1)

Her lack of a personal form of worship was not the only denial and sacrifice Esther made as queen.

A follow-up reading describes another one:

Q–2. Is there a karmic link between myself and [5766]?*
A–2. In the activities when the entity was queen, then this entity was as one who opened the doors, who was as the guard, who was as the one caring for the queen in those experiences.
Q–3. Did I once hurt him emotionally?
A–3. Not so much hurt as a disregard of the affection shown. The difference in the position after the entity was made queen caused more of the hurt.
Q–4. Why has he had such an emotional effect upon me, stirring me to such depths. I find him almost distasteful at times after a short contact, yet a glimpse of him often leaves me deeply stirred, and extremely

_____

*No personal reading was given for 5766. The number is used to preserve his identity.

lonely, why? Was he ever a knight or war-
rior? His carriage seems to bring haunting
memories, and a sort of pride back to me,
why?

A-4. Look at the conditions that must have
existed then; being almost betrothed to the
entity, then suddenly being made queen,
causing the difference in the positions. Hence
this is natural that the entity allows self to
become emotional over the variations in the
positions at present. (1298-3)

HAMAN REINCARNATED

Six months after the Vashti readings were given,
a third cameo was added to the Esther-Vashti drama.
Her new husband obtained life reading and was told he
had been Haman, Vashti's loyal advocate.

From the intense self-centeredness which Cayce
attributes to that incarnation, no doubt, came his reputation as the arch-enemy of the Jews. It never served
his purpose to favor them.

Before that we find the entity was in the
Persian land during those experiences when
Xerxes or Ahasuerus* was upon the throne,
during those periods when turmoils arose
according to the activities of Ahasuerus in the
dethroning of the queen.

The entity then was overzealous in its
own personal gains, in the name then Haman, which came to be to a portion of
those experiences as a byword; yet to those
peoples that were in authority from what
would be termed today the educational and
the purposeful view, of high estate.

In the material things the entity lost;

---

*Xerxes is the Greek name, Ahasuerus the Persian or Jewish
name for the king.

again in the mental and the soul and the influences for the greater development, the entity gained.

Beware in the present of the egotism of self becoming a stumbling block. Use rather as a constructive force, and we may find not only will the material, the harmonious mental and the greater soul development arise from those associations of those experiences there, but those activities that may be as a part of the entity's sojourn or activity in the present. (1273–1)

Esther in Power

With Esther's rise to power and the establishment of Mordecai as prime minister, the position or security of the Jews with the Persian kings was firmly established.

These readings speak of Jews raised to authority through Esther's influence.

. . . we find the entity was in the land about the peoples of promise in a strange land, during those periods when there was the raising of Esther to a position of power.

And *again* there were those activities with the Persians . . . and the rising of power, and the falling away of power of the Persian king.

The entity then was among the chosen peoples, and a *relation* to not only Mordecai but to Esther also, and came into a position of power as one that would supply not only to its own peoples but to those of the king's household, to those of the king's consorts, the entertainments, the actualities of the experiences, of the interpretation at times of the law, the applications in those experiences that brought the closer relationships of the entity's own peoples to the king and those that were in authority.

There we find the entity gaining and losing. In those same activities that made for understandings and interpretations, because of power, because of fear of those influences that would be wrought, the entity became self-indulgent, and lost for a portion of those experiences.

The name then was Carolieen. (1193-1)

This reading describes another relative raised to power.

Before that we find that the entity was in the land through the periods when the children of promise were under bondship to the Persian king, Ahasuerus.

There we find the entity was among the offspring, or household, of Mordecai—who became to the peoples of that time and place as a lord, as a prophet.

For, through the influences as may bear upon the entity even in the present, Esther brought those places of position and power to the kinsmen of Mordecai and of herself, when she—Esther—became queen.

Thus we find that in the present experience the entity may find fame and position in high places bringing to the entity in the present, even as then, those inclinations for quite questionable influences in the thoughts of self as well as others.

The name then was Te-huran. (1646-2)

Cayce's philosophy of the unity of men through the oneness of God created a point of view which was objective and universal. As much as he loved the Bible and the Old Testament Israelites, he was not blinded to their faults. With Esther's rise he commented on the characteristic pattern in the use of her power.

> "Esther is lauded as a great savior of her people, a sort of martyr to the cause. Still, we notice that after she gained power with the king, she caused the same destruction to others that she had prevented for her own people."

But What of Vashti?

Throughout Edgar Cayce's Story of the Old Testament the life readings have added many new heroes, personalities, and spiritual lessons and examples to the Bible story. Queen Vashti is added to this gallery.

Vashti is an example of integrity and morality. Like Tamar (Genesis 38; reading 1436–2), Vashti refused to compromise her soul by yielding to man-made edicts.

> Why did Vashti fail to present herself at such a condition or period? It was not only because of the political influence of those that had been placed in power, and the pitting of the friendships as one against another, but because of the moral attitude owing to the religious trend as a follower of Zend.* (1096–2)

Esther is one of the honored women of the Bible, yet Vashti deserves equal prominence for her integrity and the example of equality she gave to women.

---

*Zend, according to the readings, was a Persian incarnation of the soul who later became Jesus. Zend, the readings state, was the father of Zoroaster.

In the fourth and final reading in the Vashti series, Edgar Cayce evaluated the Vashti incarnation and its significance.

This entity came into an experience during those early activities of Ahasuerus, or Xerxes as called by the Grecians, that there might be during those experiences a fulfilling of the promises that had been made to a peculiar people . . .

In that experience, though belittled by those that were in a development of a *personal* ego, those activities of the entity filled a parallel with that universality of love in holding to that which made for the elevating of the activities of others to that which cries aloud in its seeking for expression—that all souls, men *and* women, stand as ONE before that Universal Consciousness, that Throne of grace, of mercy, that has brought the souls of men into materiality in body, that there might be an awareness more and more of *their* relationship—yea, their kinship to that *source* of right, justice, mercy, patience, long-suffering, love.

Hence the entity in that particular experience found itself in that position of championing the cause of those that had through the timidity of the activities from the expressions been kept in that way of woman being the weaker vessel. Yet in the very activity there came to the forefront that expression which found its *crowning* when the virgin gave birth to Him who became the Savior of men!

In those surroundings of egotism, then, in those surroundings of faults and fault-findings, the entity *gave* to those peoples, to the world, a concrete example of the *freeing* of the souls of those that, though in body they be joined to those in power or authority, seek—their individualities, their souls, their entities seek and make expressions in a material world! (1096–4)

Cayce told the woman that her present incarnation was for the same purpose she had served as Vashti.

That it *again* may give expression to the *freedom* of the soul even under the laws that have been made by man, for these be not the laws of the Universal Love . . .

The ideas will come, naturally flow through self . . . through the ideas and through those expressions that will naturally arise—that which will *free* man! . . .

And that man and his companion as from the beginning must stand as *one* before not *only man's* made law but as they do in God's holy law! . . .

Q–5. How may my book bring clarification in the minds of many regarding that period of Vashti?

A–5. As indicated, as held by the traditions of a peoples who have through their very urges kept alive rather the abasement of woman's position in the relations, in the activities as subservient to the orders of men, the entity may use those activities in the present to give expression to that variation that is thrown off now as having been a yoke that was set by man's vanity, not God's purposes! (1096–4)

Vashti was twenty years old when she was chosen queen, and reigned for eight years. (1096–3) After her fall from favor, she was given to a friend of the king's as a companion. (1096–2) The change was a belittling experience for Vashti and created an influence still present in the entity that causes her to question those who have dedicated themselves for an active service and do not separate themselves. (1096–3)

Even after her fall, she still was presented with choices.

> When another was chosen and the entity was to become demoted, there came the choice for those activities that held to the purposefulness of self—in keeping self in accord with those that were the moral laws of the entity, rather than enjoining with those things that might bring for the entity a position or pleasure for a season. (1096–1)

She died five years later.

> Only at the age of thirty-three did the entity depart that experience, through those activities that came about by the destruction of those that clamored against those peoples raised to authority *by* those that supplanted Vashti in the experience. (1096–2)

EZRA AND THE SECOND RETURN

Those who accept the authenticity of Esther as a historical event, dispute whether Esther was actually made a queen, or given an honored place in Xerxes' harem, because no records have yet been discovered which indicate that Xerxes had a Jewish queen.

Whatever her position was, it gave the Jews great prestige at court. Esther remained an influential person in the palace when both Ezra and Nehemiah went to Jerusalem.

Approximately twenty years after Esther became queen—about sixty years after Cyrus' first edict—the second return to Jerusalem got under way, led by Ezra.

Xerxes was succeeded by Artaxerxes who, as Esther's stepson, was also favorably disposed toward the Jews. It is generally assumed that Ezra held a high position in the court, perhaps as the king's advisor on Jewish affairs.

While Zerubbabel and Jeshua returned to Jerusalem, Ezra remained in Babylon where he earned the reputation as a greater scholar and interpreter of the law. The first return was devoted to the temple rebuilding and reviving the priesthood; the second period was dominated by Ezra's interpretation and application of the law and its effects upon the people.

Ezra was a devout reformer and strict interpreter. His approach was legalistic and exclusive; he was a "purist" in his commitment to his religion.

Conditions in Jerusalem were not rising to the expectations of the Jewish leaders, and apparently Ezra felt the situation merited his presence in the city.

> For Ezra had set his heart to seek the law of the Lord and to do it and to teach in Israel statutes and judgments. (Ezra 7:10)

Although Ezra's intentions were clear, Artaxerxes' motives were not, at least to one of his counselors:

> The entity was among those of the Persian or Chaldean land who became imbued with that causing the individual ruler, not an adherent of that faith, to issue such edicts; whether to be popular with the subjects and in following Cyrus' edicts or whether motivated by the seeking of those in authority as priests and scribes in the city of the king, when there were those requests for the prayers of the children of the king. (2940-1)

Artaxerxes approved Ezra's request to return to Jerusalem. In addition to being given the responsibility of instructing Israel in the laws of God, the king also gave Ezra sweeping authority to levy taxes, take tribute, and appoint judges and governors throughout the region. Artaxerxes also gave great treasures to Ezra from his tribute and out of his own household to be used for the refurbishing of the temple and as purchase for needed supplies.

Because of his scholarship and devotion to the law, Ezra was looked upon as its representative and chief example. He took his position seriously, and lived not just with tenets and ritual, but with a serious and practical application of the prophetic ideal, both in Jerusalem and on his way there.

As he set out on his journey, Ezra felt it incumbent upon him not to ask for a Persian military guard. He was "ashamed" to ask for a military escort because he had said to the king, "The Lord is with those who seek him for good." (Ezra 8:22) If Artaxerxes looked upon the Jewish activity as a religious experiment, as his father Xerxes did (see 1297–1), the sight of unaccompanied Jews marching across a hostile, and in parts lawless, territory with a great amount of booty must have created rich philosophical speculation.

Ezra was living what he believed. He trusted the revelations of the prophets, and was doing what he knew was God's will. Although he could easily have been annihilated, or at least humiliated by bedouin outlaws or village chieftains, after a four-month march Ezra and his people arrived safely in Jerusalem.

EZRA IN JERUSALEM

When Ezra and his troop arrived in Jerusalem, the princes came and informed Ezra of the conditions in the land, emphasizing particularly the vast amount of intermarriage between the Jews and the people of the land. Ezra was overwhelmed and aghast. This strict and literal interpreter of the law was stunned and shocked by this terrible news and "sat speechless" until the ninth hour, while those who were "diligent concerning the word of God" assembled around him and gave their interpretations and versions of the situation.

After hearing all their views, Ezra was moved to pray for mercy. The law of Moses forbids intermarriage, and violation of this law had been Israel's undoing in the past. Ezra felt that the grace God had been shown by permitting a "remnant" to survive, in spite of the great sins of their ancestors. The opportunity to rebuild, Ezra believed, was now jeopardized by this great sin.

REFORMS

Ezra's prayer was long and infused with the strength of sincere conviction. Although he himself was not guilty, he included himself in the petition as he prayed for God's mercy and forgiveness. Perhaps his inclusion of himself among the sinners added to the strength of his prayer, which made such a deep impression on the leaders and people who were present.

When Ezra arose from his knees, he had made his decision. Only by breaking up the foreign marriages could he get at the seat of the sin. The people were asked to repudiate their foreign wives. When many did not, Ezra took drastic measures to separate the mixed couples. A committee was organized with the laborious task of investigating all the cases in the land. The investigation was carried out over a period of three months, and met with division and opposition in some quarters. But many were moved to join with Ezra and his reforms.

During the Babylonian captivity, many Jews had intermarried with Chaldeans, and then Persians. The peasants, who had been left in the land to care for the vineyards and trees (2 Kings 25:22), had taken foreign wives. Those who had remained in the land had seen the temple destroyed and national unity broken and had become prey of the pagan peoples. Many of them had given up all hope of any restoration. These people had children and grandchildren.

Now they were being asked to repudiate their wives and exclude their loved ones from the Jewish community. The human anguish and heartache in Ezra's harsh policies cannot be measured. The testimony in the Books of Ezra and Nehemiah indicate this hard line met with some success, but other testimony (Nehemiah 5) shows it caused great hardships. Many were aroused to a new vigor and dedication in observing the prophetic ideals, but it also caused a disspiriting and a demoralization of a large number.

Edgar Cayce made an enlightened observation to the Bible class about Ezra's reforms.

> "He was a learned man, who had been educated in a foreign land while in captivity. When he came home he began to make application of some of his knowledge, but as applied to the letter of the law according to the old records he found. Ezra didn't try to modernize the terms of the law to fit the changed environs. Some of his strict rules of conduct were, no doubt, as strange and foreign to the people of that day as some of the rules of the Puritans would be for us now, in our modern times. Naturally, this caused trouble."

This reading bespeaks of the hardships of personal experience, yet spiritual development also, from that edict.

> In the one before this we find in that period when there the entity was among those who labored in the rebuilding of the wall ... The entity gained in the greater portion

of this experience. Hence that peculiar phase of religious fervor that has permeated the being of the entity, or the body-being in the present; faltering oft, as it was in that experience, through the various activities as were brought as for the contentions as arose in marital relations, as the contentions arose in that experience through the sojourns with individuals where the relationship had brought, did bring for that experience, that made for separations under conditions and circumstances that brought trials, tribulations and ordeals to the body. In the name Myriah.

In the present experience from this, we find added *with* the fervor of religious thought, sacredness of certain relationships with individuals, and those—to the entity— that break their word, or their bond with others, are as those that would do bodily harm to others. Hence the moral, religious, and the *filial* relations of the entity, are high —and oft have they received *in* the experiences those of desecration. (2141–1)

LOST RECORDS FOUND

Ezra's great interest in the law and his interpretations which characterized this period could, in part, have stemmed from phenomena described in the readings, but unaccounted for in the Bible—the discovery of "lost" records in the temple ruins. The effect of these discoveries cannot be measured, but the impact must have been catastrophic. Individually, as the life readings will show, the study of these records affected, and changed, many lives. Historically, it must have added to Ezra's determination that the law should not be just hearsay or tradition, but something to be applied and lived, leading to the great emphasis on translation and interpretation during the Ezra-Nehemiah period.

This part of Edgar Cayce's Story of the Old Testament begins with the woman who discovered the lost records:

> Before that we find the entity during those periods when there was the returning to the Holy Land.
>
> It was during the return of the second group, when the activities of Ezra and Nehemiah made for the greater gatherings of the peoples that would return to the worship in the Holy City.
>
> The entity then was among those that were very close to those that served as a portion of the temple activities.
>
> Thus it came to be the more interested in the redecorations, the rehabilitations of the hangings of the temple; as they went about the repreparations.
>
> And to the entity may be accredited the discovering of the portions of the writings that were later transcribed by Ezra.
>
> For the entity CLEANED in the temple when they were discovered. Is it any wonder in the experience that there is continued to be unfolded to the entity, in its seeking for that which is the pearl of great price in the experiences of others in their attempts to make for the greater manifestations of the love of the Father as shown to the sons of men?
>
> The name then was Rebekka. (1456–1)

The lost records, apparently, had to do with conduct regarding the priests, as seen in the following. The study of these rules added to the spiritual climate, and changed this entity from within.

. . . when the first of the groups returned to the holy city with Zerubbabel. The entity was among those, being a companion to the priest, Eleazer.

The entity then was in the name Juduth. The entity was one who helped prepare again the priestal robes for the people in that first period of preparation, taking from the records which were again discovered there, and thus the entity brought to self, brought to the many, a greater knowledge of the closeness of the Father-God to man in this new period of activity.

Thus in the present, not overzealousness of the Lord, or the word of the Lord, but the innate ability of being pleasant, of being consistent, of being in that place of not finding fault with others. This is a lovely experience and don't be afraid, there's not but few that have that consciousness as ye have in thyself. But don't abuse it, don't misuse it! For it is of the divine. (5241–1)

Because of the many groups which had been scattered in foriegn lands, as well as the Jews who had remained in the Holy Land and intermarried, and those who were in Babylon, a variety of languages and dialects were spoken. In order for the law to be understood, it was necessary for it to be interpreted. Children born of the mixed marriages spoke the language of the mother, which was a dialect of the Hebrew tongue. The Moabites, Ammonites, and Edomites were akin to the early Hebrews, and spoke different Semitic dialects. Nehemiah and Ezra both were opposed to the mixed marriages and the departure from the Hebrew tongue.

Yet the readings describe a great effort to put the law into the language of the people as well as to coordinate all the history and records into the Hebrew. A dual activity is described in this reading:

> There the entity was as the COMPANION of the scribe, Ezra; making those activities which brought into the experiences of the young what might be called the re-establishing of the school—that had been a part of Elijah's experience on Mt. Carmel.
>
> For, the entity aided those who set about to make the copies of the law, the interpreting of same into the language and into the dialects of that day.
>
> Hence the entity made for advancements throughout that experience, AS the teacher then, in the name Luenar.
>
> In the present application from those activities, the entity will find that EASILY there will be recalled much of those things that were as ordinances—especially that had been neglected by those who were teachers AND interpreters through their period of exile; and as to those things and activities which had been a part of same. (2444-1)

The new discoveries led to a closer study of the law. The study created in this entity a firmness of conviction, which brought her into conflict with the authorities.

> The entity was then among those who aided in the establishing of the original activities of the priest, and the entity was one among those who worked upon the garments of those who ministered in the temple.
>
> In the name then Marian, the entity was given to the building up of the body, mind, and soul and failed not in its administrations

to the many offices; though questioned even by the scribe of the period and Nehemiah, as he later appeared on the scene, but the entity's help brought conclusion to the activities as the law was studied the more closely by the entity, as well as the associates. (4055-2)

The intense study of the discovered records led to unexpected benefits for several entities who were involved in this important work. Talents for linguistics, interpretation, translation, and ability to work with groups of diverse backgrounds were carried into the present incarnation.

A reading for a Tennessee housewife describes her life in Jerusalem:

The entity came with the last group, or those portions under Nehemiah; known to those leaders, Ezekiel, Ezra, and those that became the greater active in the recording of the records.

And we find the entity then, though in the opposite sex from the present, was among the scribes and translators of those activities during that experience; and associated with those in the temple as well as in those activities that gave the ministry in the teaching, the interpreting, the changing of the law as befitted the language of the day.

Hence we will find in the present the entity is a good linguist, one easily able to learn or to interpret other languages. The associations of the entity with peoples of various tongues will be a part of the experience. Yet the letter of the law and the spirit of the law not only of man but of God becomes a reckoning, or an experience or a judgment to be made by the entity in this present experience . . .

Then the name was Shulemite, of the tribes of Judah AND Benjamin combined; for the entity made for an advancement, development, materially and mentally and spiritually during those experiences. (1499–1)

A reading for a one-month-old child shows where his abilities lie.

There the entity was as an aide to Jeshua, as well as Ezra, in the interpreting of the law to the language of the peoples of that period.

Hence we find the entity will be inclined to language, and especially the study of same; an excellent reader, an excellent interpreter of the old and the new writings. These will be the natural inclination of the entity.

The name then was Eloieh. (2498–1)

This reading shows another talent related to language stemming from this period. A California woman was told:

The entity was among those who were the early births in that land, and in the household of Ezra, the scribe, as his daughter by Athelie—and the name of the entity through that sojourn was Astedoth.

The entity aided much in the interpreting of the parchments or scrolls that were found, translated, and written for the peoples of the period.

Thus the entity in the present would find the abilities to WRITE—EVEN YET*—of those things, conditions, and experiences

---

*She was eighty-two years old at the time of her reading.

which would enable individuals and groups
to see and to foster and to cherish the BET-
TER experiences in their activities through
this material plane. (2305–2)

Any new discovery can, as the Lord's Prayer says,
"lead us into temptation" or "deliver us from evil,"
depending upon our use and application of the knowledge.

This entity, of the first return, saw the law discovered and heard it interpreted. He gained a great
vision mentally, but lost spiritually when he tried to
force his vision on others.

A present-day student of Theosophy was told:

. . . the entity was in the Promised Land
when there was the return from the land of
the Persians—and with Zerubbabel the entity
came into the Holy City—saw the desolation,
and the raising up of purpose in the hearts
and minds of individuals through the experience; and saw and heard the interpreting
of much of the law as was discovered among
the ruins of the temple.

Hence the entity through the experience
became one well-grounded, materially, in ritual and rote for a purpose of purifying body
and mind, as same was designated or dedicated for any individual activity for many.

The entity gained, the entity lost through
that experience—as Adonajahem. For as the
entity gave and let others give also, it gained.
As it attempted to impel or to prevent those
not so endowed with the broader vision from
their class or environ, or by the heritage of
the environs in a strange land, the entity lost
—as it hindered others. (1703–3)

One great phenomenon which has occurred throughout man's spiritual evolution is the uncovering of "lost" and forgotten information. An undisclosed amount of ancient wisdom is embedded in the earth in a variety of forms. It remains hidden until man is ready for its discovery.

The Cayce readings describe a secret chamber near the feet of the Sphinx, as yet undiscovered, which contains the history of Atlantis and the teachings of the Law of One. When these are brought to light and interpreted, they will revolutionize man's religious concepts and his view of the past. Yet the readings intimate that only an initiate in the knowlege of the One God can unseal the chamber (5750–1), and will, when mankind needs and is ready for the information it contains.

In Joshiah's time, the lost books of Moses were discovered because Judah needed them in order to "preserve a remnant" to keep the lineage of the Promised One. Under Ezra, when Israel was again zealous in its desire for God, lost records were again discovered, almost as a symbolic show of God's presence.

The Bible itself was a "lost" record, except for an educated handful, until the invention of the printing press. When the masses in Europe began to get pages and fragments—seldom the whole Bible itself—translated into their spoken tongue, it created a revolution, and a vast reorientation in religious beliefs.

The earth, with the storehouse of hidden knowledge it contains, is an outward expression of man's own subconscious mind, which, as the readings tell us, contains all the wisdom of the universe and a record of all our experiences as a soul. The Christ has promised to bring to remembrance "all things from the foundations of the world." Thus, new discoveries are brought out of the depths of the mind by the spirit of

God, supplying what information we may need from day to day.

EZEKIEL IN JERUSALEM

The influence of Ezekiel and his prophecies is widely recognized as an essential factor motivating and inspiring the tiny remnant to rebuild and rededicate itself to God. His unique contribution to the history of prophetism lies in his manifest interest in the temple and the liturgy, an interest unparalleled by any—including Jeremiah, who was also a priest. His influence on the postexilic religion was enormous. He has been rightly called "the father of Judaism."

His first prophecies prepared Israel for the destruction of Jerusalem, and his later ones held up the promise of salvation through a new covenant and the conditions which were necessary to obtain it. The exiles were the only hope of Israel's restoration, once the allotted time of exile had been fulfilled.

However, the readings suggest another dimension to Ezekiel's involvement with the postexilic community which is unaccounted for in the Bible or in any Biblical traditions.

The readings refer to Ezekiel as a leader of one of the returns. (1732-2, 1759-1) Readings 1434-1 and 1499-1 indicate that it was the second return, with Ezra.

In a reading for a child we find:

> The entity [was] among those who ministered to the needs of the ailing and the sick, and was the physician in this period to Ezekiel—who led this return. In the name Zedkahi, and the entity gained and lost through this experience—gaining in the application of self to those who labored in the cause; losing in the selfish stand as taken against those who persecuted the builders—

and brought to self condemnation for self in the attitude assumed. (759–1)

Whenever there is a threat or a danger menacing, there is also a greater Presence available which can overcome it. Ezekiel, as a teacher, instructed his scribe how to avail himself of that Presence:

> In the one before this we find [the entity] in those days when the walls of the Holy City were being repaired under that direction of Ezekiel, and the entity coming in, then, from that of the king in exile, and was then the assistant to Ezekiel, as the scribe, and the entity gained in that plane, for under the tutelage, the power of the force as was manifest in Israel, the entity assisted much to those who labored on the wall, who defended the helpless from the invasions of those who would hinder. Then in the name of Abidda, and the urge in the present is that closeness as is felt to all things sacred ... (257–10)

Another follower of Ezekiel is described here.

> ... when the peoples of the promised land returned to that land from the exile, and under the leadership of Ezekiel did the entity return to the Holy City, and among those of the household of Zerubbabel. The entity gained through this experience; giving self much in service of those who labored in the restoring of the Temple and in the aiding of those who gathered of the worldly goods to make same possible, both from the house and lands of Artaxerxes and also of the lands about the Holy City, being of the household of those that warred with Sanballat during this rebuilding. In the name Corienl, and there

were *many* that called the entity *blessed* during that experience. (1732–2)

One individual who was told he had been "a messenger to all the realm" during the Creation cycle in Genesis, in his next incarnation was very close to another messenger—Ezekiel—and later was Jude, the brother of Jesus.

In the one before [the Jude incarnation] we find in that of the one calling the chosen people from the Assyrian lands to the building again of the walls of the Holy City, and this entity in that of the armor bearer for Ezekiel. (137–4)

EZEKIEL'S VISION

Ancient Astronauts and a Flashback to Atlantis

And, remember, man—the soul of man, the body of man, the mind of man—is nearer to limitlessness than anything in creation. (281–55)

Because man is a soul, and the soul is nearer to limitlessness than anything that is, the theory, popular today, that ancient astronauts came in spaceships in the early days of man's evolution to educate and guide him in planning new civilizations, is no longer necessary to explain the existence of highly advanced prehistoric civilizations with superior and highly sophisticated technologies and theologies.

Man's first existence was a soul, a spiritual being in the image of God, and, according to the Edgar Cayce readings, his first contact with the earth plane was in this condition. The material plane became, for spiritual man, a laboratory into which he could project and experience his own creative abilities. The contact with materiality gradually sapped his energies, distracted him, tempting him to further separate from his spiritual estate. The more materialized and encased in dense, gross three-dimensional forms the soul became, the greater was the atrophy of creative ability and loss of awareness and memory. Man devolved until he reached his lowest point, and then began the slow ascent upward, back to his spiritual source.

A soul is eternal, and through the fall in spirit, has need of regeneration through the process of many incarnations in the earth—a process and an opportunity sanctioned by a merciful God of infinite love.

Who were the ancient astronauts? *We were!* Superior beings also came with blueprints for a new civilization, and then depart. *They're still here!* We are those ancient civilization builders, the legendary scientists, technicians, astronomers, priests and poets, and spaceship commanders of fabled prehistoric civilizations. Our abilities are not "lost" but forgotten and lie within, waiting to be awakened through the realization of our full creative potential.

If this is an explanation of the past, what explains the present? Are the UFO sightings today a form of visionary experience, the results of a psychic dislocation in the Collective Unconscious, as suggested by Carl Jung? Are they purely fabrications and hallucinations? Or, literally, "men from outer space"? Are they, perhaps, fellow souls, who are experiencing life in a different dimension of consciousness—our sons, daughters, brothers, parents, friends, and neighbors who have walked upon this earth but are now in the "inter-between" and no longer bound and limited by the flesh?

These questions serve as a prologue to a discussion of Ezekiel. Ezekiel is one of the most mysterious of the major prophets. His prophecies, advices, and exhortations provided much of the inspiration and determination of the Israelites to rebuild, yet little of what he said and did is studied outside the seminary. But one portion of his experience is widely known and cited most often as evidence of extraterrestrial contact with visitors from outer space. (Ezekiel 1)

> *And I looked, and behold, a whirlwind was coming out of the north, a great cloud, and a flaming fire and a brightness was round about it, and out of the midst of it there came as it were a figure out of the midst of the fire.*
>
> *Also out of the midst of it came the likeness of four living creatures. And this was their appearance: they had the likeness of a man. (Ezekiel 1:4-5)*

Was Ezekiel visited by men from outer space, as a popular theory suggests? Or were the great, flashing spinning wheels of his vision (Ezekiel 1:15–21) a glimpse, while in an altered state of consciousness, of the *chakras* of his astral body, as suggested in esoteric traditions? Was the vision purely a hallucination, or a fabrication, as gathered from the rationalistic, materialistic point of view?

Several levels obviously apply.

From one Edgar Cayce reading, we have an indication that the symbology, or the experience, could have been drawn from memories of an earlier incarnation.

In a life reading, we find this description:

> Before that we find the entity was in the Atlantean land, during those periods particularly when there was the exodus from Atlantis owing to the foretelling or foreordination of those activities which were bringing about the destructive forces.*
>
> There we find the entity was among

---

*The Deluge, according to the readings, was the second destruction of Atlantis. See *A Million Years to the Promised Land*, Chap. 5.

those who were not only in what is now known as the Yucatan land, but also the Pyrenees and the Egyptian.

For the manners of transportation, the manners of communications through the airships of that period were such as Ezekiel described of a much later date. (1859-1)

Another clear indication of Atlantis-derived symbology appears in the prophecy against Tyre. (Ezekiel 28:12-15) The references to Eden and the conditions described by Ezekiel clearly have their parallels in the Cayce readings on Atlantis, the site of Eden.

If the Spirit was reaching into Ezekiel's mind to articulate its message—why would it not activate—in a prophecy of destruction—the memory of the greatest destruction, Atlantis, and overlay it on his message to Tyre?

Ezekiel attuned himself to the great storehouse of God's Memories, the Akashic Record, and the symbology and prophecy which flowed through him was channeled for the benefit of his and all future generations, each to find, in its multi-leveled meanings, the revelation that speaks to the soul.

Yet the study of "memories" does not exhaust the possibilities. Another interpretation in the readings suggests Ezekiel's vision may have been from his own subconscious (or superconscious) mind with a message, in part, as a warning to himself.

For a man with pronounced psychic potential whose development had been guided through a number of readings, Cayce gave the following interpretation of this dream:

Dream: An aeroplane rose in the sky trying for height, and for height only. Aeroplane came to a sudden and disastrous stop. Starts its sudden crash for the earth, leaving a wake of flame from fire. Plane seemed to be in

231

the vicinity of Mt. Washington, a light mountain in the White Mountain Range . . .

Edgar Cayce: This, we find, is the emblematical condition as was given to Ezekiel, as found in [the] last half of first and second chapters, as called. This, we see, pertains to the mental of the individual body [137]. And the altitude, or heights, in the place, we find showing the place where there might be the giving of popularity through such manifestation [of psychic ability]. The sudden descent and the blaze of fire is of the destruction that it would bring to self, if the popularity were the thought in mind, and in [the] expression to the populace or peoples. This, then, is as the warning that would come to the one who would attain great heights in the psychic forces as obtained through such manifestations. (137–10)

BREAKING DOWN FROM WITHOUT

The renewed interest in the law and the discovery of the old records engendered great mental activity, leading to the formation and implementation of new interpretations and policies. The great problem was the race question, which potentially was the most destructive and explosive issue challenging everyone.

Although Ezra's policies were harsh and uncompromising, his approach was needed to convince the people of the importance of their heritage and purpose; yet, at the time, his policies created great upheavals which almost destroyed the community itself by dispiriting and demoralizing a large segment of the populace.

God creates, not by bringing about uniformity, but by creating diversity which then requires a greater degree of integration.

God unites, and evil divides. Selfishness and egoism made reconciliation difficult, but reconciliation was the one prerequisite for survival. Reconciliation requires that each side give up something in order that reconciliation may take place. This takes place when enough people will be guided by the Spirit within, which is forever seeking unity, harmony, and brotherhood.

Ezra injected a necessary element into the struggling community, and Nehemiah, who followed him, became the reconciler. Thus the work progressed as an organic whole, with each individual making his contribution.

The most destructive adversary (from without) was Sanballat, the principal resister who, with Tobiah the Ammonite and Geshem the Arabian, is mentioned in the Book of Nehemiah. The self-righteousness of the priests, who refused the mixture people's joining in the beginning, was also spiritually harmful in its effect upon others.

This life indicates the effects of the rejection:

> The entity was among those who had been left in the land, and was that one who with Sanballat sought for a consideration among those efforts attempted.
>
> Because of the refusal of those in authority, there came distresses and disturbances, and those attempts to placate the activities. Again there were the attempts to establish in the mountains the worship as had been proclaimed by other teachers.
>
> Hence there were the doubts and fears of those who were self-righteous. Thus in the present we find the entity is one who within himself dislikes self-righteousness, and who becomes wary of those who by might or power would proclaim or INDUCE others to be forced under their rule or their guidance.
>
> The name then was Joseph. (2167–1)

This reading describes the discord in one of the "mixed" race:

> The entity was among those who grew up in the land—those who were not taken away, and the entity joining with those in the return was pulled many ways; for having been once a consort in Sanballat's group (not personally), the entity found much that brought consternation in the material affairs, yet harkening most to those spiritual instincts and gaining something of the spirit of those who would rebuild . . . the entity became an extremist, pulled from one to the other—even as is seen in the present, often halting between two opinions; yet in presenting any condition, position, thing, person, place, or time that the entity has set self to do, this entity does! In the name Bennahi. (1915-1)

This one was left in doubt and confusion:

> The entity was among those peoples who chose to come with the first under Zerubbabel, yet the entity was not wholly of the Jewish or Hebrew blood. And these very influences made for confusions when the entity made overtures or associations with the friends and associates of Sanballat or those who had been left in the land and known later as the Samaritans.
>
> This among the entity's own close associates caused confusion and disturbance. (1523-4)

Another indication of a disrupted family is shown in 2344-1:

> Before that the entity was in the Chaldean land, when there were the gatherings of those

under the king to be returned to the land of promise.

The entity's companion sought rather to remain, and yet under the supervision or counsel of the friends as related to Zerubbabel, Ezra, Nehemiah and the leaders in the return, the entity persuaded him to join with those who did return. And this brought to the entity some doubts as respecting these conditions, when turmoils arose with the neighbors in that land.

Hence we find the entity then was being halted between two ways, yet in the application of self in those manners that made for the unifying of the purposes—even under the stresses of the occasions, the entity found peace and happiness. The name then was Uslar. (2344-1)

Life reading 2153-3 shows more turmoil for one close to Zerubbabel:

The entity then was among those close in the household of those who directed that activity, under the direct lineage of Zerubbabel, of the Levites—and thus of those of the priesthood.

In the beginnings the entity aided much, but with those disputations which arose regarding others who are descendants of those left in the land, the entity sided more with those [the descendants]; and thus brought disturbing forces in its experience, and . . . rebellion . . . The name then was Esdreldia. (2153-3)

THE RESISTERS

. . . each individual must stand according to that he has applied—and not according to class, or heredity. In other words . . . merely being in power, or power alone, does not always make right. (1638-1)

. . . for innately the entity is spiritual minded, but being blinded by those of power of possession, of the abilities to say "Come and he cometh," these may be turned into those of destructive forces for the entity. (1234-1)

The principal opponents of the rebuilding were Sanballat the Samaritan (Nehemiah 2, 4, 6), Tobiah the Ammonite (Nehemiah 4, 6, 13), and Geshem the Arabian (Nehemiah 6). Although Ezra must have encountered difficulties with these men, he makes no mention in his writings of them or any source of trouble which led to the breakdown of the work. Nehemiah, on the other hand, designates who the chief resisters were, and pinpoints other problem areas, such as the merchant's disregard of the sabbath law and intermarriage. (Nehemiah 13)

Sanballat, Tobiah, and Geshem made every effort to stop the rebuilding, conspiring even to kill Nehemiah, who they also accused of rebellion against the king of Persia. (Nehemiah 4)

Although Ezra's hard-line policy may be criticized, it was done with a positive purpose in mind, enabling him to make an enduring contribution to the welfare of mankind.

Those who resisted had only destruction as a goal. Sanballat's name appears frequently in the readings for this period, indicating he was the most formidable antagonist, the one whose "destructive forces" impressed themselves most strongly on the minds of the people. His rejection by Ezra and Nehemiah must have been galling to his ego, and created a party factionalism within the Jewish ranks. (Nehemiah 13) One of Jehoiadah's descendants, the priest who had been

Joash's guardian, was the son-in-law to Sanballat. (Nehemiah 13:28) This son-in-law was Eliashib, a high priest, who also gave a place to Tobiah the Ammonite in the court of the house of the Lord. (13:7)

The following reading speaks of the destructive purposes of the resisters. In an early life reading, we find the armor bearer to Sanballat.

> The entity then among those who resisted those that builded, being in that [name] of Sanbad, the armor bearer to Sanballat—and the entity lost through this experience, for those that builded builded in a purpose. Those that resisted did so for the satisfaction of the self and for the power that might be given to self through that of destructive forces to man, and that the builders represented. Bringing to self destructive forces through aggrandizement of selfish interest. The urge as is seen from same, that of mistrust in some that build toward selfish motives, even though the appearance is good. (165–2)

This reading suggests the devastating effect Sanballat had upon the people.

> . . . as the wife of a brother of Zerubbabel . . . the entity aided then in making for strengthening of purposes in the hearts of those who labored under such circumstances that brought fear and trembling, owing to the various causes roundabout, the activities of the sons of Sanballat and the peoples without the gates and the peoples that were left in what later came to be known as the mixed races—those of the Samaritans. (1033–1)

This one again indicates the seriousness of Sanballat's threats. As "the wife of one of the Korahites":

> The entity gained through the associations and relations, giving much to those peoples that were so tempted by those peoples roundabout who under Sanballat and his kind tempted, and tempted, those that would serve . . . The entity in the latter portion of that experience became a teacher and an aid to the establishing again of the schools for the prophets . . . (2118-1)

BREAKING FROM WITHIN

The readings indicate that Ezra's hard line almost caused the rebuilding to fail. His attitudes toward intermarriage led to upset and turmoils among a great many of his people, even among the pure-blooded, not all of whom agreed with his policies.

In other areas his strict interpretations clashed with the perceptions of others and led to additional discontent, and a siphoning of energy into conflicts, when unity was desperately needed.

Eventually, under Ezra's regime, the work had to be stopped because the people were "discouraged or disheartened" because of "the rebellious forces roundabout" and from "turmoils and quarrels from within." (2006-1)

A reading for a Polish rabbi describes an incarnation as Zerubbabel's son, and an episode which brought to a halt the labor on the walls.

The entity was rebuked by Ezra, and he rebelled:

> . . . we find the entity was in that period when there was the return of the children of promise from captivity to the rebuilding of the walls of the city, to the rebuilding of the temple itself.

Then as Zuekide, the son of Zerubbabel, the entity labored at the rebuilding; and was set as one of the sons who kept and gathered the tax that was to assist in the re-establishing of the temple service.

The entity then, being overzealous as to those activities, was rebuked not only by those under Nehemiah but those in the second return—as Ezra.

Hence those things recorded as of Nehemiah's and Ezra's writings have in the entity a feeling of insecurity, insincerity; for the rebuke was deep to the entity. For had not the entity felt that those who were able to pay *should pay* for those who were *unable* to pay?

Hence the *innate* feelings were higher even than the priesthood; and the entity was banished, becoming among those that—as it were—followed from afar. Yet the entity aided mightily with its bodily strength in building up the city, in building up the walls roundabout.

No wonder, then, that these have a peculiar feeling for the entity; yet at times one of repulsion, and again the feeling that there are those things mightier than the walls which bespeak the efforts of man in those directions to set up that which may be sustaining as a momument—that should be builded rather as the lowly Nazarite gave, "Not in this mountain, nor in this city; rather in the hearts of men, should the God of Israel be worshiped." For He has given, as through this entity then, [that] there is not required silver nor gold nor only sacrifices; but there comes the call that ye be just and patient and long-suffering with thy fellow man. For *these* bespeak the words of Jehovah rather than those that require this or that rule.

And it was because of such a rebellious force of the entity that they ceased to labor on the walls, until Nehemiah came. Yet with a mighty labor did the entity give of the strength in that experience . . .

Hold fast to that thou didst gain before the altar in the temple; that God loveth mercy and justice rather than ritual or might; that being patient, being kind, being gentle is more precious in the sight of Jehovah than the offering of many sacrifices or the giving of bounty, or the requiring of this or that of the law itself. For who is the law? He that loveth mercy and justice, or he that ruleth in the thunder or in the might? *God* is a God of love!

These things gave forth the entity; these ring true in the experience today. (991-1) [Italics added]

Those who made a big show of proclaiming and interpreting the law were under close scrutiny by this entity. Their example created dissatisfaction, which added to the breakdown of the community:

Under Zerubbabel did the entity first enter, and also under Nehemiah did the entity labor. In the name Gehgin. The entity gained through this experience, yet the religious experience of the entity during this experience was not altogether satisfactory to the entity; for the lives of many as leaders, the lives of many as priests, the lives of many of those that waited on those that were of the house, of the temple, were not in keeping with that held *by* the entity as compatible with that they professed. Hence the entity in the present experience, hard to judge, hard not to condemn, hard not to say the life is not so and so; yet the broadness of vision as respecting religious experience is gained through *this* experience. (99–6)

The breakdown of cooperation and unity is again suggested in the following:

> Before that the entity was in those activities that followed the return of the children of promise to the Holy City, when the activities were brought about by Nehemiah in the third of the drawings upon the crowds.
>
> Then in the name Samantha, the entity became associated with those who labored in and about the temple. The great stresses laid by the varied leaders at that time brought a characteristic to the entity that is apparent in its present personality: when others dispute among themselves the entity chooses its own way and goes along without considering any. And these are the periods when the entity is misinterpreted, or judged on the one hand as knowing much more than it gives expression to, and on the other hand as being not just exactly in the same line that it would pretend in thought.
>
> These are the experiences. Not as faults, but as misapplication at times of a virtue that is apparent from the experiences through that particular period when the entity contributed to the welfare of others as a nurse and as a physician. (3478–2)

In a reading for a young soldier we find a reference to conflicts between the priests. Apparently there were differences over ritual and worship, as well as the mixture people:

In the activities the entity saw those disputes that arose between the priests of one class and those under Ezra and Zerubbabel and Jeshua.

Hence in the present we find those questionings as to ritualistic activities of any particular faith; yet the entity in its contribution to the welfare of the peoples in that period united much of the efforts; not only of those who had been left in the Holy Land but those disputations that arose because of the mixing of the races—or of the peoples of the land with the children of those returned from captivity.

The name then was Adonjhed. In the experience the entity was a looker-on, as might be called, and yet a contributor to the welfare and the activities of peoples—as indicated in the universal consciousness of the entity . . . (2940-1)

Help came from an unexpected source. It was not a priest or religious leader who responded, but a civil servant, a citizen—Nehemiah—who was touched and stirred in his heart. Nehemiah was the king's cupbearer, and was one in whom the king had absolute trust and confidence. Poisoning was, and still is, common in the orient. Therefore, the cupbearer had to be the most trusted official in the king's retinue. The Persian rulers, being despots and lavishly wealthy, had many enemies. No one, not even members of his family, could be trusted.

The cupbearer was also one of the few with whom the king could be intimate. Persian kings lived in complete isolation. Not even the queen or his children could approach him without being summoned. The cupbearer could come freely into his presence, and was one of the very, very few who could be personal with the king.

Thus, when the king observed Nehemiah's sad countenance and asked about his depressed mood, Nehemiah was able to speak freely.

". . . why should not my countenance be sad, when the capital city of the kingdom of my fathers is in ruin, and its gates have been burned with fire." (Nehemiah 2:3)

The king responded to Nehemiah's concern, and granted him all he asked to carry out his mission: military force, supplies, and royal authority.

And the third expedition was underway.

13

The Third Return

The Book of Nehemiah opens with an account, by emissaries from Jerusalem to Nehemiah, of the deplorable situation in the Holy City:

> *". . . Hanan, one of my brethren, came, he and certain men of Judah; and I asked them concerning the remnant of the Jews who were left of the captivity and also concerning Jerusalem.*
>
> *"And these men whom I asked said to me, The men who escaped captivity, behold they are in the city, dwelling in misery and reproach; the wall of the city also is broken down, and its gate has been burned with fire." (Nehemiah 1:2, 3)*

Commenting to the Bible class, Edgar Cayce made the following observation:

> "The men gave Nehemiah a sad report concerning the work in Jerusalem. Whether this great affliction had come because of Ezra's strictness regarding the marriage law, or from the disputes which had arisen with the people roundabout, we do not know . . .
>
> "We wonder if being such a great moralist didn't redound to Ezra's harm in the end.

However, he must have felt what he was doing was right. Most of us at times choose wrongly, but if we are willing to acknowledge it and ask God, we can be sure of having the correct way pointed out."

NEHEMIAH REINCARNATED

The amazing consistency and cohesiveness of the entire Cayce material is again found in Edgar Cayce's story of Nehemiah. In a reading for an elderly businessman, still alert, active and aggressive at seventy-six, an incarnation as Nehemiah is described. In the reading we find these qualitative descriptions about the entity in the present, all of which stem from his expressions in former incarnations:

One that knows most of the time what it desires, and sets about to gain same . . . one democratic in its ideas and the freedom of thought, the freedom of activity, the freedom of choice—and that the answer must ever be within the individual self to give the reason for this, that or the other choice of activity in its experience . . . One tender-hearted in its dealings . . . One inclined to give credit where credit is due . . . One that must ever keep romance as a part of its everyday experience. (1767–2)

Leadership ability was acknowledged.

. . . the entity is considered as the leader and the director in many an undertaking of every nature or character. A natural builder of character . . . (1767–2)

The character and nature of an entity, or soul, varies little from incarnation to incarnation. Change and development is builded "line upon line, precept upon precept" not just in one lifetime, but over many. Thus the consistency of this soul is shown throughout— a uniter of diverse loyalties, and a respecter of the individual conscience. As Nehemiah, the entity was a leader and able to unite those who were willing to "work for a purpose."

Before that we find the entity was again in the activities of the builder, when there was the second and third return of the people of promise from the lands where they had been in exile for so long.

There we find the entity was the leader, the lawyer, the soldier, the director—Nehemiah.

And if there will be the perusal of those things that are considered as the messages of Ezra, as well as those of the activities accredited to Nehemiah, we may find much that is responding to something within as to the desires and purposes of the entity even in the present experience.

The abilities as the builder, the abilities as to judge, as to the thought and as to the ability of producers in ANY field of service.

And as the entity then sought to give example to those over which the entity had authority, those who were willing to work, those who would work must be willing to work for the purpose and to work with and never FOR the entity or the individual, but work with, toward the building of something within the mind, the heart, the soul of each entity for the GREATER purpose for which each soul finds expression in materiality!

So from those experiences there are the abilities in the present as the leader, as the director—the ability to listen as well as to give the orders. These are innate and manifested in the experience of the entity. (1767–2)

The reading described an incarnation following the Nehemiah experience during the Constantine period when the Roman church began exerting its influence. As a result of his incarnation as Nehemiah in the Holy Land, where law and order and personal conscience were the important underlying issues, the entity saw church and state clashing over whose authority should govern. The entity was able to see both sides in the disputes, but his position was the same as it had been in the past and was in the present:

Yet for the entity, the basis of that taught by Him *is* that the Way, the Truth, the Light may be free for all, and that the choice in the present, as then, must be within the individual rather than that as may be given as authoritative by any group or individual who would act in the capacity of a director. (1767–2)

The whole reading supplies the basis for an interpretation of the differences between Ezra and Nehemiah. Ezra enshrined the laws, the rules that should govern man, whereas Nehemiah favored man himself.

Ezra gave the unique and characteristic stamp to Judaism and preserved a nation, and a heritage; but Nehemiah appears to be more representative of the universal spirit, found in Jonah, Ruth, and the early visionary experiences of Abraham, Noah, and Jacob.

Another aspect in this reading, which also demonstrates the total consistency of the Cayce spiritual interpretations, is that each incarnation prepares us for the next. Our future lives are conditioned by our activities in the present.

The atmosphere created by Ezra—divisions and

factionalism—could only be resolved by a soul with the ability to unite diverse elements into a working whole.

The life reading shows that Nehemiah's abilities were developed in a preceding incarnation in ancient Egypt. The Egypt of this period was one of rebellion and upheaval. It was an era of "turmoils, strifes, and divisions."

Cayce described the entity's contribution to an unsettled era:

> In the experience the entity it might be said saved that period of activities for the great work that was accomplished in the land by unifying all those in the political, the social, the religious influences during that sojourn. (1767-2)

The "great work" alluded to above was a reference to the spiritual and religious developments which took place under the priest Ra-Ta, after the civil war and rebellion were settled. Thus, in the following incarnation, the soul was attracted to the Holy City and the Jews, and a similar situation in another important period of man's spiritual advancement.

The reading concludes:

> ... the entity may give in this experience, may be in the unifying of the principles of law, order—but under the spiritual and purposeful guidance for each soul to be accountable unto its own conscience to that call which rises from within as to its relationships to the Creative Forces or God, as may be expressed by its dealings with its fellow man. (1767-2)

Nehemiah's personal influence is an essential part of his story. Men worked for and with him because of their love and respect for the man and his goals. The readings add to this picture of his magnetism and charisma.

Cyrus' daughter (3351–1) is described as in love with him. Another individual, a member of the Babylonian court, was told that she had been his "lady friend." (3271–1)

Two wives are also attributed to Nehemiah. The first wife was a Chaldean, thus making Nehemiah guilty of "mixed marriage."

> The entity was active in that particular portion under Nehemiah, or the one known as or called Nehemiah; for the entity then was the companion or the wife of Nehemiah—in the name Adjaah, being of the Chaldean as well as of the Jewish peoples.
>
> In the experience the entity gained throughout. While there were periods of turmoils and periods when many anxieties were brought for the entity because of the mixed relations, the entity developed because of the adherence to and the fulfilling of not only the records for the king but for Nehemiah. (1612–1)

While the first wife was of the mixed race, but gained spiritually, Nehemiah's second wife "lost." The tone of this reading suggests she may have been a pure-blooded Jew, perhaps taken by Nehemiah as a conciliatory move toward Ezra's faction.

> Then, the one before this, we find in the return from the captivity in the land to the

promised land. The entity then in that of the one that was the aide to the one leading the peoples, for the entity then the wife to Nehemiah, and the entity then lost in that appearance, for the desires were to the land and not to the service. This *again* we find is felt in the inner self in the present, that these are the rule—that the head of the house should rule, yet the assistant, or the mate, should have [her] word. (2486-1)

Another woman, a companion in the past, was drawn to this same entity again:

Then in the name Shelehi, the entity was a companion of Nehemiah—that has been, *is,* a companion of the entity in the present. (1144-2)

THE PERSIAN GUARD

The moral and financial support of the Persians is shown in the Bible story, but their actual involvement with the work in Jerusalem is not so clearly indicated. Here the readings throw an illuminating light, adding a universality to the work that is not indicated in the Scripture. Jews and Persians worked side by side. Apparently Nehemiah made full use of a source of help which had been unthinkable to Ezra.

This reading tells of a Persian soldier, an architect, who was drawn into the work because of his admiration for Nehemiah:

The entity then was among those who worked close with Nehemiah, for the entity was of the Persian peoples who aided in the replenishing, having accepted the activities because of the love of the entity for that leader.

Hence as a soldier, as well as a builder or an architect or an engineer, the entity—as Azuriel—was active in strengthening the determinations of many of those peoples who were under the supervisions of that entity through that particular sojourn. (2162-1)

We find in this reading that Artaxerxes' nephew accompanied Nehemiah on his return.

Before that we find the entity was in that land now known as the promised land, during those periods when there was the return from captivity to the rebuilding of the walls and the temple in Jerusalem.

The entity then was not of that peoples now called the Jews, but rather of the Persians; being then a nephew of Artaxerxes, and of the household of the rulers of that land, yet so closely associated, so closely active with those forces under Nehemiah that the entity was the representative then of the Persian peoples that went with Nehemiah for those activities in suppressing the influences that had arisen that caused the stopping of the rebuilding of the walls.

So again we find the entity associated in what would be called in the present means, ways, and manners of communications for messages that must be sent to those in authority in Babylon . . .

There may be yet discovered those activities of *this* entity, Axterern, in the excavations that are being made in portions of what is called Mesopotamia, for the means for preservation of messages—that was a part of the entity's activity.

In the experience the entity gained, because of those promptings of the king to let those peoples go that cried for a means of expression, a means to return to the material activities in a spiritual service to that as was held by them to be the way and means of serving their God . . .

Hence those latent forces that make for the tenderness—as may be called—in the entity's experience; the tenderness of heart, and the willingness to listen to a sad story, the ability to make those expressions of sympathy —not only in words but in deed. (1362–1)

THE KING'S RECORDS

The Persian kings throughout this period showed great interest in keeping informed about events concerning the Jews and the rebuilding. Persian letters and documents are important elements in Ezra and Nehemiah.

. . . the entity was in the promised land when there were those edicts given by the Persian kings for the return of those children of promise; that they might themselves establish their OWN worship according to their own ideals.

The entity was an armorbearer to the king; and eventually was sent as one to assist in seeing that those edicts were carried out, and that protection was given to those who labored in a cause.

Thus the entity came into the promised land with Nehemiah, with Ezra, Zerubbabel, and those who labored in those periods of activity. From there the entity reported back and forth. There the entity kept the activities in such measures that from one king to another there were the various edicts given that

aided those peoples to again establish a place
of worship.

The entity gained and the entity lost
through those periods of activity. Hate arose
because of the attempts within some of those
to turn the activities into self's own interest;
until those periods when there was the establishing of that necessary for the rebuilding
of the wall, in which there were the edicts by
the entity that the weapons of defense be
kept at hand, as well as the implements with
which to repair the wall. (1662–2)

Another reading speaks of the king's interest:

The entity was among those who came
into the Holy City with the activities of Nehemiah, when there were the gatherings rather
for the rebuilding of the walls and the making
of the covenant or the pacts or agreements
with the peoples roundabout. Also there were
to be reports made to the king—yes, kings—
who had given the decree or who had allowed
these peoples to return for their own religious undertakings . . . (1583–1)

Another record keeper is described here:

For the entity, though being rather of the
Persian than of the Jewish peoples, was
among those who joined with the activities
for the preservation of peace, as well as the
keeping of the records for the king who had
given the decree or made it possible for these
people to return to their Holy Land to set up
again their activity—yet being under the supervision, as it were . . . of the Persians . . .
(1539–2)

This reading tells an interesting story of a Persian official who overcame the dissipation of court life through the hardships in Jerusalem:

> In the one before this we find in that period when there were those returnings of a people to the Holy City, and among or with those under Nehemiah did the entity journey from Chaldea to the Holy City, being among those that directed the movements of the peoples— both as the representative of the king and of the peoples that would replenish, resupply, resuscitate—as it were—the *moral* and material relations of a people to carry on ...
>
> The entity gained through this experience, and lost and gained; for with the setting out the entity rose to power; with the humdrum that came with the lack of those elements to supply the same surroundings the entity entertained and enjoyed in the king's favor, dissipation came, discontent arose, and the entity lacked [stamina].
>
> With the finding of those relationships in others that brought for a better understanding, though hardships ensued in many ways the entity found self and aided in giving to the peoples much strength to withstand those foes without as well as from within.
>
> The entity was then in the name Cerrabil. (1932–1)

NEW POLICIES

Although Ezra and Nehemiah were in agreement on their purposes in Jerusalem, their methods inevitably had to vary. The differences in their character and personality were marked. Ezra was a "religious idealist" and Nehemiah a "practical realist." Whereas Ezra was "ashamed" to ask the king for protection,

Nehemiah was willing to use whatever help was at hand. Ezra had a mystical concept—the prophetic ideal —which he was trying to realistically implement. Nehemiah, one feels, was more involved with the human situation and the needs of his fellow creatures. Ezra felt man had to meet and live up to certain preconditions, while Nehemiah accepted those who had the "right purpose" even if their religious or racial backgrounds differed from his.

Ezra was a man devoted totally to his religion, while Nehemiah, it appears, was a political and social, as well as religious, creature.

Nehemiah's approach was practical and logical. He must have evaluated the situation in Palestine and the Holy City, and then requested the king for the necessary authority to remedy the problem areas— even if it meant overriding some of Ezra's dictums.

Nehemiah was empowered to make "covenants and pacts" with the outside groups:

> The entity was among those who came into the Holy City with the activities of Nehemiah, when there were the gatherings rather for the rebuilding of the walls and the making of the covenant or the pacts or agreements with the peoples roundabout. (1583-1)

The Persian kings were interested in keeping peace in this area, and were concerned with the natives and their reactions to Jewish policies.

This individual was to report on the situation:

> The entity was among those who were of the groups that came with Nehemiah, when the walls were to be rebuilded—though the associations of the entity were with the peoples who had come under Zerubbabel and the laborers of those who were in command, or under the direction of Nehemiah as with

the priest and with the scribe—with whom
the entity was associated because he had received a decree from the king that there
should be kept the records of the activities
not only of those who were in authority *but
as to how well the activities of that people
were received by the natives as well as the
remnant as had been left in that land.* (1933–
1) (Italics added)

Apparently the king wanted to keep all his subjects as content as possible, as well as allowing the
Jews "freedom of expression."

For the entity, though being rather of
the Persian than of the Jewish peoples, was
among those who joined with the activities
for the preservation of peace, as well as the
keeping of the records for the king who had
given the decree or made it possible for these
people to return to their Holy Land to set up
again their activity—*yet being under the supervision, as it were,* such as the entity represented, *of the Persians,* or during those
periods of the Medes and Persians. (1539–
2) (Italics added)

One reading uncovers what might have been a
real source of conflict between Ezra and his adherents,
and Nehemiah and his followers.

Nehemiah had the legal power to override Ezra
in formulating policies to maintain peace. Thus, reading 2970 tells us, when the walls had been rebuilt
there was "the *re-establishing* of the relationships with
those that had been disturbed because of the intermarriage with the peoples of the native lands." The
reading continues, and seems to suggest Ezra, or other
leaders, ignored and failed to support these measures:
"Yet by those in authority, much of these were set

aside, to the undoing—or misinterpreting—of many."
(2970–1)

Which is greater—the faith of the idealist, or the wisdom of the realist? This was the crux of a question raised in the mind of this entity as he observed the two leaders and the implications in their behavior:

> The entity then was an aide to the peoples as they returned; coming first with Zerubbabel and aiding with those under Nehemiah. There the entity saw under varied activities; the one disregarding the influence from without, relying wholly upon the spiritual promise from within that they would be cared for, yet with the Nehemiah influence the entity saw those activities wherein there was the trusting to the power of might, to the name of the king, to the effect that this must produce upon those lands and peoples through which the first of the bands under Nehemiah passed.
>
> Then in the name Jeel-bached, the entity gained; for the entity held close to those things that became the precepts with those activities under Zerubbabel.
>
> Also the entity saw the greater application of those activative forces that impelled the writer of same to say that the work progressed because they all *had a mind* and a purpose to work, to serve a living God! (633–2)

The readings answers the question: *Be true to your own guidance!*

> These should be *ever* those influences prompt the activities of the entity in all its relationships, drawing more and more upon the meeting of that great I AM Presence, as

257

it was given to the fathers of old, "Whom shall I say hath sent me? I AM THAT I AM!"

When these influences are relied upon, in the experience of him who has set his house in order, then such an one may indeed be guided aright. Do not rely upon the fleshpots of Egypt, nor the places of the high hills, but rather in *humbleness* of purpose serve the Lord; for He is good. (633–2)

A CHANGE IN STATUS

Although Nehemiah is one of the most beloved of Jewish leaders, we find in this entity one who hated him because of "revolutionary edicts" he proclaimed:

Before that we find the entity was in the Holy Land during those periods when there were those returnings from captivity when there were the activities of Ezra, Nehemiah, and Zerubbabel. The entity was among the daughters of Zerubbabel, who entered into the temple service and yet, with the periods when there were the upheavals brought about by the changes when Nehemiah made those revolutionary edicts, the entity swore vengeance. And he who swears vengeance pays even unto the last farthing. So it brought developments, retardments, for when there is jealousy, hate, things that do not make the soul of man free, these bring retardments to an individual in his activities in the earth. The entity was in the name then Adar. (5177–1)

Evidently Nehemiah was fearless in his effort to get at the source of the problem—questioning even the highest officials about their policies and activities, including the direct descendant of the royal family. This entity had come with Zerubbabel, and as "royal blood" perhaps he was overzealous in breaking up the mixed marriages:

> Before that . . . we find the entity was among those of that period when there was the returning of the children of promise from alien lands to the rebuilding of the walls about Jerusalem, and the temple that was first begun—under Zerubbabel.
>
> For the entity, while not of the priestly family, was rather among the sons of Judah; and in direct lineage of the king that had been carried away captive—Zedekiah.
>
> In the name then of Zedder, the entity's activities were in keeping the accounts of its own peoples as related to the edicts that had been issued by the king of the Persian land.
>
> The entity made for a development in those in many respects; only losing when there became *questionings* under the leaderships as brought by Nehemiah.
>
> Hence we find the entity in its religious turns and religious activities often questions those who are put into authority for delegated activities of church or church relationships to definite activities . . .
>
> In the present the entity may gain much from those experiences by the study of those things presented not only by Nehemiah but by Ezra. For these will, in a great measure, recall to the entity innately; and gradually manifest in the experience of the entity itself those activities during that sojourn. (1120-1)

More general discord between Ezra's group and Nehemiah's is indicated here:

With the rebuilding of the temple and those activities under Zerubbabel the entity first came to the land. The divisions or disputations which arose among the second and third groups who returned brought disturbance and disorder into the experience of the entity, yet the ability to plan, the ability to become very staid or set or hardheaded, all arise from the experiences of the entity then as Perthuel. (5358-1)

The change in the balance of power brought with Nehemiah was a welcome one to this entity, who was in disfavor for acting on behalf of the mixture people.

There we find the entity was with the first of the groups under Zerubbabel that came into the land.

There we find the entity acting as the intercessor for those peoples of that later called the Samaritan land, and the attempts to make for those periods when there would be a united effort in the rebuilding.

Losing in the efforts and activities there, the entity lost faith, lost "face" with those leaders—until there were those activities under Nehemiah that brought the greater numbers and the altering as to the relationships of individuals . . .

Hence we will find in the present experience that any building of wall or any activity of the nature holds an interest for the entity; as also does the study of that which will bring UNION out of the devious manners of thoughts of various groups.

The entity will oft be asked to act in the capacity of the peacemaker . . .

The name then was Abdjah—of the children of Judah. (1842-1)

"Water Gate" suddenly erupted in our contemporary situation with a force and impact which will not soon be forgotten. Yet "Water Gate" is not new. It appears in the Bible, in a situation of some relative significance to the present.

Then all the people gathered themselves together as one man into the street which is before the water gate; and they spoke to Ezra the scribe to bring the book of the law of Moses. (Nehemiah 8:1)

In a prolonged and determined effort of fifty-two days, Nehemiah and his Persian troops, and Jewish supporters, rebuilt the walls of the city, thus insuring its safety, and the safety of the people within, from attack and invasion by the outside resisters. The wall was the practical solution to the problem which was coming "from without." With this work completed, there would be time to turn to the problems within. Internal consolidation and reform were made possible by the reconstructed wall.

When the walls were complete, Nehemiah ordered that a genealogy of all the people who participated be recorded.

Following that, the people gathered before the Water Gate and asked that Ezra read them the law. And at the Water Gate the extremes met. The many moods, attitudes, understandings, and misunderstandings that were in the people were gathered in one place.

Based upon his understanding of the psychic material which had been coming through the life readings, Cayce saw this eighth chapter of Nehemiah as the place where Nehemiah and Ezra "locked horns," though, as he told the Bible class, "it is not recorded that way."

If Cayce is right, and Ezra and Nehemiah did "lock horns," the issue was probably over the interpretation of the law. Up to this time the people had never read or understood the law for themselves, but had been getting other people's interpretations and proclamations. Now they were to understand it for themselves.

> *And Ezra blessed the Lord, the great God. . . . Also Jeshua and his sons . . . and the Levites ministered to the people explaining the law; and the people stood in their place.*
> *So they read in the book of the law of God distinctly, and gave the sense, so that they understood the reading thereof. (Nehemiah 8:6–8)*

The teachers and interpreters read and discussed each topic until it was understood by those who listened. Edgar Cayce suggested they must have met in small groups where questions were asked and answered until all became of "one mind" and agreed to the sense of the meaning.

It is interesting to note Jeshua's name heads the list of the interpreters. He was the one who had copied and rewritten the Biblical history from Genesis through Nehemiah, and was the one whom the readings state was Joshua, Joseph, Melchizedek, Enoch, and Adam.

The people wept as they heard the law read. (Nehemiah 8:9)

Mr. Cayce spoke to his class:

> "Why did the people weep? Because they recognized they had gotten far away from the law. It had never been interpreted for them before. They had heard what was considered to be the essence of the law, which had been handed down to them. But now they began to realize that the law was something to live, just as we are having to learn at this time."

After they understood the law, the people confessed their sins and entered into a new covenant. Those who took the oath were recorded. A tenth of the people were chosen by lot to dwell in Jerusalem and the rest in the outlying towns. The temple service was reorganized and the walls dedicated, and a program of vigorous reforms was instituted, such as halting the wanton disregard of the sabbath by many of the merchants.

The spirit of the community had fallen to a dangerously low ebb. Selfishness had made its deteriorating inroads, dividing and fragmenting the people through a variety of issues and causes until the original intent and purpose for the founding of the nation and its rebuilding had been lost.

Before that we find the entity was in these periods when there was the return of a chosen people to their land for the reestablishing in the land of promise of a ritual service.

There the entity, with Zerubbabel's handmaids, became a helpful influence. And with the coming then of the priest—or princes —and the prince in Nehemiah, we find the entity lent that aid which made for the helping of those who resisted the peoples roundabout. Not by might, not by power, but by lending a helping hand to those who suffered bodily; aiding in bringing to those a better understanding of that edict which was given by the king for the reestablishing of those services of a peoples in their *own* land.

Then the name was Belenda, and the entity gained, lost, gained through the experience. For being misjudged for the associations with those then as of the heathens roundabout, as termed by those strangers in their own home land, the entity felt within self as being misunderstood and condemned, when innately within self there was known how the protection was brought even to many of those that labored upon the wall, as well as in those that were established.

Yet if the entity will read very closely the sixth and eighth chapters of Nehemiah, it will find much that harkens for an awareness of its presence there.

Hold to those things that make for this ability to be tolerant, even with those that despitefully use thee. For it engenders strife to hold animosities ... (1143–2)

The reading of the law and the successful attempt to have the people understand it was the saving grace through which unity and solidarity was achieved. Ezra's interpretations, while good for many, did not speak to the well-being of all. Although a great reformer, Ezra could not unite or rectify the many diverse moods his policies had created. Nehemiah was able to reconcile the extremes and create a new synthesis and harmony out of many diverse elements.

Through the public reading of the law, everybody worked together until they all could agree and get their own understanding. Renewed through this experience, they became unified in their willingness to work for a common goal, a common ideal. Spiritual renewal and reform, which had been so essential throughout Judah's history, worked again to preserve the nation and insure its continuity.

AT THE WATER GATE—THEY WERE THERE

At the Water Gate, this entity learned the meaning of the law. A psychology teacher was told:

Before that we find the entity was in that land when there was again the preparation for the return of the chosen to the temple and to the Holy City.

And the entity with Nehemiah and Ezra came into the activities, in the Holy City, from the Persian and Chaldean land; and was an aide to Ezra in the interpreting of the revising of the law as then found.

Thus in the present there is the opening of the understanding as to how the interpretations of tenets are things to be *lived* and not held as tenets or as rote alone!

For as ye have learned, it is even as He ―who "went about doing good."

The name then was Shes-Beder. (1529–1)

This entity's understanding of the law enabled her to be a peacemaker:

The entity was among those that were born in captivity, to be sure, yet joined hard with those peoples not only that aided in giving comfort and aid to those that went with Zerubbabel but with Nehemiah in his return with political influence and force.

For then the entity represented not only the law of his peoples but the law as an edict of the king, then changed.

These made for those experiences when it may be said there was the greater development of the entity in a material, in a soul, in a mental experience. For the application of the law as interpreted and read by Ezra in the hearings of the entity, then Abajah, produced in the activities of the entity the making of the first overtures to those about the activities in the city when the temple had not only been rebuilt but when the walls had been rebuilt, that made for peace and harmony.

Hence the entity in its activities while as a law interpreter, as a lawgiver, as a law devisor in ways and means, will ever be in the capacity rather to make peace than to stir up strife among peoples or groups or nations or states. Thus the activity in that same capacity in the present may bring the greater development, bringing the greater harmony and peace into the experience of the entity in the present. (1285-1)

In this reading we find a resister who changed sides:

Before that we find the entity was in the Holy Land, when there was the returning of a peoples to those activities in a rebuilding of the walls, and the repairing of same, and the restoring of the temple.

There we find the entity was among those peoples who warred against that general activity, yet becoming—in the second and third dispensation of the king who made it possible for those people to return—a part of same.

The name then was Abijah, and the entity in the experience was warring with self as to principles; and being under the influences of Nehemiah, the leader, brought an influence for power for good throughout the experience. (1998-1)

This entity, of the mixed race, gained from Ezra's interpretations:

The entity was among those who were the offspring of those left in the native land, and hence there was a longing for and yet withdrawing from those of that environ where organization had been attempted.

And thus with the return of Zerubbabel and those activities under Nehemiah, the entity came again into an active service; and yet brought discord through the attempts to unite the efforts of Sanballat with the peoples who had journeyed from the land of bondage—or of outcasts.

There we find the entity learned, little by little, those variations in the law of the period and the experience; and only under the interpretation of Ezra did there come the more perfect understanding for the entity.

Thus we find in the present it behooves the entity to first know self, and know the ideal, and know the sources and the purposes of same; and the abilities for the making of associations with toilers of the soil in all of the phases become the abilities in the present.

Then in the name Eljah, the entity lost and the entity gained. (1946-1)

A high note resounds in this reading for an entity of the mixed race who rose above all the turmoils to an honored place in the temple service:

Before that we find the entity was also in the Holy Land, as known in the present, during those periods of the return of the peoples of promise.

Though the entity was of those peoples that remained in the land, it became especially interested because of the activities which followed the intents and purposes of the edict issued by Ezra during those experiences. And as the entity showed itself to be equal to and sincere in its efforts for the establishing of ideals, it was among the very few chosen to become a part of the experience in the re-establishing of the temple and the spiritual worship of those peoples during that experience.

The name then was Belenhi. Though among the Samaritans (as called), and of that people, the entity gave its service to those who made for the establishing and re-iterating of the laws pertaining to the service and the activities in the temple, and the activities of the peoples in their replenishing and reactions in those experiences.

The entity gained then throughout.

In the present we find the ability to interpret, the ability as a linguist being a part of the entity's experience, from those VERY abilities as established during the retranslating of much of those things that were a part of the experience.

And if the entity will review the activities of Nehemiah, Ezra, and Jeshua and Jezreel, much of these will become as an opening door to the consciousness of its abilities to direct, to hold, to maintain a UNITY where others have failed.

Thus the entity will be enabled to give even the greater counsel to those just starting their relationships as one with another, and with the EFFORTS in fitting themselves into environs and activities in which they have found and do find their experiences entirely different from their earlier periods of activity. (1663–2) (Italics added)

THE ETERNAL LIGHT

And God said, Let there be Light, and there was light. (Genesis 1:3)

Out of the darkness of chaos and disunity, the people merged into a new totality by searching for the one light that could guide their ways.

With the rebuilding of the temple, we find this entity a keeper of the lights. Apparently the temple lights were symbols of the "eternal" light which never fails or grows dim, and shines even in the darkness when man neglects and forgets.

The entity, in the present, finds the eternal "inner" light illuminating his visions and dreams.

> The entity then among those of the latter peoples that returned under Nehemiah, and the entity then one that kept the lights in the temples in the city, and the first of the lights that might be kept burning without the continued attention were set *by* the entity in *that* period. In the name Zeruri. The entity gained through this experience, for service in the capacity as the *keeper* of the lights—in the directing forces as was given by Nehemiah, as was given by Ezra the priest, as was given by those in that period—brought an understanding and a knowledge of the associations of *spiritual* forces with *material* forces, and the entity happy throughout the experience—from the leaving of Shushan* *in* Persia (now) to the promised land [and] the holy city. In the present, as will be seen, oft does the entity vision, by the various lights and the odors as arise in the imagination, those of the various experiences as in the way through the desert, through the hill land, as well as the visions in the cities, and the *dreams* of the entity oft partake of *those* experiences. (2662–1)

---

*The royal residence of the Persian Kings.

The great period of rebuilding, with all its struggles, its strifes, its divisions and differences, was completed because the light which all these diverse entities were seeking—Jeshua, Ezra, Nehemiah, Zerubbabel, and the many others—was greater than the darkness which separated them. That same light still shines, able to draw all men into unity and brotherhood, if all men will search for the spirit from which the light proceeds.

BACK TO THE BEGINNING

Resettling the promised land, and rebuilding the temple, made it abundantly clear to the Israelites that the days of the monarchy were finished. Only the inward unity and solidarity of a religious community could guarantee their existence in the face of whatever world and political developments might confront them in the years ahead.

Israel was returning back to the beginning. Israel turned its back on politics and great worldly ambitions. The high priest became the head over all Israel. The little community was no longer a monarchy, but a theocracy, as it had been in the days of Samuel, the priest and prophet who warned Israel that their demands for a king were "sinful."

With Persian approval, the law of God became the law of Israel. For two centuries the Persians were the liege lords of Jerusalem. Israel kept apart. Archeology indicates no violent variations during this period. There were no plottings, no machinations, no rebellions. Only an outward quiet or calm, and an inward searching for purpose and direction.

With the rising of Alexander, the Macedonian empire supplanted the Persian. Again, Jerusalem kept free of entanglements and involvement, in a shifting and changing world. Jerusalem was untouched by the invasion of Alexander as he marched on Tyre and Egypt. Indeed a legend exists that Alexander intended to sack and destroy the Holy City, but changed his plans when he realized the high priest of Jerusalem was the same man he had seen in a dream before leaving Macedonia. Alexander turned aside and spared the city. Perhaps this story is only a legend, but it serves to emphasize the fact that as long as Israel kept to the things of God, no harm of any nature would come to them.

There is very little in the sacred writings about the four-hundred-year period between Ezra and Nehemiah and the birth of Jesus. Nothing important happened in outward affairs, nor were there great manifestations or revelations from God.

Yet the peace, the quiet, the unbroken continuity of purpose, over four centuries in this little religious community, enabled a sect within Jewry—the Essenes —to complete the Old Testament by bringing into the earth that which had been in the beginning—a living soul unspotted and unstained by the world, at-one with the light and in harmony with the Father. In the garden, Adam had been a "living soul," innocent of earthly experience. In Jerusalem, he became "a quickening spirit," having passed through, and overcome, all the forces, drives, and temptations that separate a soul from its source.

Ye say that there were those periods when for four hundred years little or nothing had happened in the experience of man as a revelation from the Father, or from God, or from the sources of light. *What* was it, then, that made the setting for the place and for the entering in of that consciousness into the earth that YE know as the Son of man, the Jesus of Nazareth, the Christ on the Cross? Did the darkness bring the light? Did the wandering away from the thought of such bring the Christ into the earth? Is this idea not rather refuting the common law that is present in spirit, mind, and body that "Like begets like"? As was asked oft, "Can any good thing come out of Nazareth?" Isn't it rather than there were those that ye hear little or nothing of in thine studies of same, that dedicated their lives, their minds, their bodies, to a purpose, to a SEEKING for that which had been to them a promise of old? Were there not individuals, men and women, who dedicated their bodies that they might be channels through which such an influence, such a BODY might come? (262–61)

Epilogue

THE PERFECT BODY

The soul looks through our eyes and feels with our emotions. Spiritual awareness is developed through the factors in all five senses. (487-17)

In the beginning, Man was made a living soul. The Garden of Eden is a symbolic picture depicting his first estate. Both the Old and New Testaments tell us we are gods in the making. And Edgar Cayce tells us why—because we possess a soul.

Man lost his spiritual awareness when he became blinded by material things, and self-indulgence. Having lost the original oneness, man would have to gain it back by the use of his free will, expended in the search for God.

Edgar Cayce stressed that it was just as important to understand the Old Testament as it was to understand the New. No one is perfect in the Old Testament. They searched for God, dedicated themselves to Him, tried to the best of their abilities to serve, yet they were enmeshed in all the forces that distract and tempt man, that make him proud, vain, fearful, weak, and wicked; that harden his heart, deafen his ears, and blind his vision. They were in the world, struggling to overcome all its drives, temptations, and distracting influences, yet were never completely successful until the first Adam who led Israel as Enoch, Melchizedek, Joseph, Joshua, and Jeshua became Christed as Jesus and totally Spirit-directed. Through his life in the earth as Jesus, he gave to Israel (the seeker) a new pattern, a new vision, a new consciousness for which there is found no parallel in the Old Testament.

As with him, the Old Testament is not complete until it is completed within. Mankind is still caught between the drawing pull of the Spirit and the desires of the flesh. While caught in the struggle, we inevitably repeat the Old Testament patterns. As long as we are struggling and seeking, we will find in the Bible some character or situation relative to our state of growth and awareness.

THE PERFECT MIND

Edgar Cayce tells us that, on the metaphysical level, the Bible from Abraham to Christ can be interpreted as a symbol process of mental unfoldment. (281–63) The spiritual meaning of Abraham is *Call*. (262–28) Christ is the attainment of the Call. If the story of Abraham through Christ is a pattern of mental development, then the Old Testament is the story of the building of the perfect mind—the mind that was in Christ.

Christ-consciousness—perfect awareness—is the crowning development in the pattern of Israel's growth. The growth is contained in two principles Cayce assigns to the word *Israel*.

All who seek are Israel. (262–28, 2772–1) The first principle is that Israel seeks Truth. (5377–1)

There is a specialized connation to Truth as defined in the readings. It is described in the "A Search for God" series as "that which makes one aware of the divine within each and every activity." Truth, then, is an awareness of divinity interpenetrating and permeating all phases of life. It is a process of growth, felt on the mental, physical, and spiritual levels of the self, and takes place in each and every individual. (262–81)

Truth is an experience, and it is this which Israel is seeking.

The second principle of *Israel* is *Service*. According to one reading, the greater meaning of *Israel* is: "Those called of God for a service before the fellow man." (587–6) Or, as another reading states: "For in Zion thy names are written, and in Service will come Truth." (254–42)

The symbol and manifested reality of these two principles of *Service* and *Truth* is shown in the Christ as he applied them throughout his Old Testament incarnations. These were the building blocks of his messiahship. The people Israel, by attuning to these same principles, created the environment through which this perfect pattern could be wrought.

Like Adam, we all have fallen from the perfection symbolized by the Garden. Like Christ, we must become priests, prophets, and ministers not only for the life and resurrection of our own souls but for the benefit and uplift of all humanity.

Cayce tells us that in order to obtain "the Mind of Christ" we must, in the physical plane, be able to manifest His Spirit. Mind is the Builder, and thus we must ever seek to make our perceptions of spiritual truth physical realities. Jesus himself tells us we must become "perfect." (Matthew 5:48)

To become "perfect" entails a discipline of Mind, for we must learn to increase and expand the dimensions of our awareness from the physical through the mental to the spiritual. As "seekers" heeding our call, we are seeking a deeper penetration into the realm of ideas, to the source and father of all our energies through all the levels of consciousness that separate us from understanding that we are "the divine image" affirmed in Genesis. We are *Israel* as we seek comprehension and a new relationship to those eternal truths and processes which are embodied in the symbology of the Old Testament.

According to the Cayce readings, we were all souls in the beginning—spiritual beings in a spiritual world. This is the Eden we have lost and forgotten. Just as Genesis preserves a memory, the Revelation points to future consciousness, a potential experience for all. The Bible then is the story of man's journey from the garden to the city, from Eden to the New Jerusalem. (Revelation 21:2)

God *gave* us the garden, but man must *build* the city.

The city of Jerusalem grows in meaning throughout the Old Testament story. It was the home of Melchizedek, a spiritual center to which David gave new significance when he established it the capital of his newly emerging kingdom. After Solomon completed the temple which David had planned, he turned his energies to rebuilding and transforming David's city into a place of awesome magnificence and splendor. Jesus enlarged Jerusalem's meaning when—as a symbol —it became the seat of his kingdom—which was not of this world!

All that was temporal and corruptible in Solomon's glories has passed away, but the city of splendor which he created inspired the symbol in the Revelation of the New Jerusalem. Unlike Solomon's city, the New Jerusalem was "a city not built with hands." It was a city not built with the taxes and forced labor a despot exacts from his people, but, like the garden, by the thought of an All-Merciful Creator.

And we find John the Beloved was the first to enter.

A NEW HEAVEN, A NEW EARTH

And I saw a new heaven and a new earth; for the first heaven and the first earth had passed away, and the sea was no more.

*And I saw the holy city, the new Jerusalem,
coming down from God, prepared as a bride for
her husband. (Revelation 21:1–2)*

Both David and Solomon had glimpses of "a new
heaven and a new earth." They envisioned things which
men had not yet seen in manifested form. When they
built, they gave to Israel a new revelation into the nature of God and His relationship and faithfulness to
those who call on Him. But, because their vision rested
partially on material things, the full understanding did
not emerge except through John.

When Jerusalem was destroyed in 70 A.D., symbolically the last vestige of the old materialistic cycle
was completed. The destruction was coincident with the
emergence of the new understanding that came with
the teachings of Jesus, David's heir.

One cycle was completed and another began,
structured on the same pattern with the same symbols
—the promised land, the Holy City, the Temple—but
on a new level of consciousness. And those who prepare
themselves by building through Old Testament patterns of searching for Truth and serving God were able
to receive the New Testament realizations of Oneness
and the free flow of Spirit in all phases of Life.

The kingdom of God, the Holy City, and the temple were established in the outer world, now they must
be built within.

This is affirmed in this interpretation by Edgar
Cayce:

Q–5. What is the meaning of "a new heaven
and a new earth: for the first heaven and the
first earth were passed away . . ."?
A–5. . . . Can the mind of man comprehend
no desire to sin, no purpose but that the
glory of the Son may be manifested in his
life? Is this not a new heaven, a new earth?
For the former things would have passed

away. For as the desires, the purposes, the aims are to bring about the whole change physically, so does it create in the experience of each soul a new vision, a new comprehension.

For as has been given, it hath not entered the heart of man to know the glories that have been prepared, that are a part of the experiences of those that love ONLY the Lord and His ways . . . For those who come into the new life, the new understanding, the new regeneration, there IS then the new Jerusalem. For as has been given, the place is not as a place alone, but as a condition, as an experience of the soul.

Jerusalem has figuratively, symbolically, meant the holy place, the Holy City—for there the ark of the covenant, the ark of the covenant in the minds, the hearts, the understandings, the comprehensions of those who have put away the earthly desires and become as the NEW purposes in their experience, become the new Jerusalem, the new undertakings, the new desires. (281–37)

Index